Xtreme Comparisons

Arctic Tern

Killer Whale

Space Shuttle

Spitfire VI

HMS Victory

Nautile

Volcanic eruption

About the author
IAN GRAHAM studied applied physics at the City University, London. Since becoming a freelance author and journalist, he has specialised in science and technological subjects.

About the artist
MARK BERGIN was born in Hastings, England, in 1961. He studied at Eastbourne College of Art and specialises in historical reconstructions, aviation and maritime subjects. He lives in Bexhill-on-Sea with his wife and children.

SALARIYA

Published in Great Britain in 2010 by Book House, an imprint of
The Salariya Book Company Ltd
25 Marlborough Place, Brighton BN1 1UB
www.salariya.com
www.book-house.co.uk

ISBN-13: 978-1-906714-56-7

© The Salariya Book Company Ltd MMX

1 3 5 7 9 8 6 4 2

A CIP catalogue record for this book is available from the British Library.

Printed and bound in China.
Printed on paper from sustainable sources.

Visit our website at **www.book-house.co.uk** or go to **www.salariya.com** for **free** electronic versions of:
You Wouldn't Want to be an Egyptian Mummy!
You Wouldn't Want to be a Roman Gladiator!
You Wouldn't Want to be a Polar Explorer!
You Wouldn't Want to Sail on a 19th-Century Whaling Ship!

PAPER FROM
SUSTAINABLE FORESTS

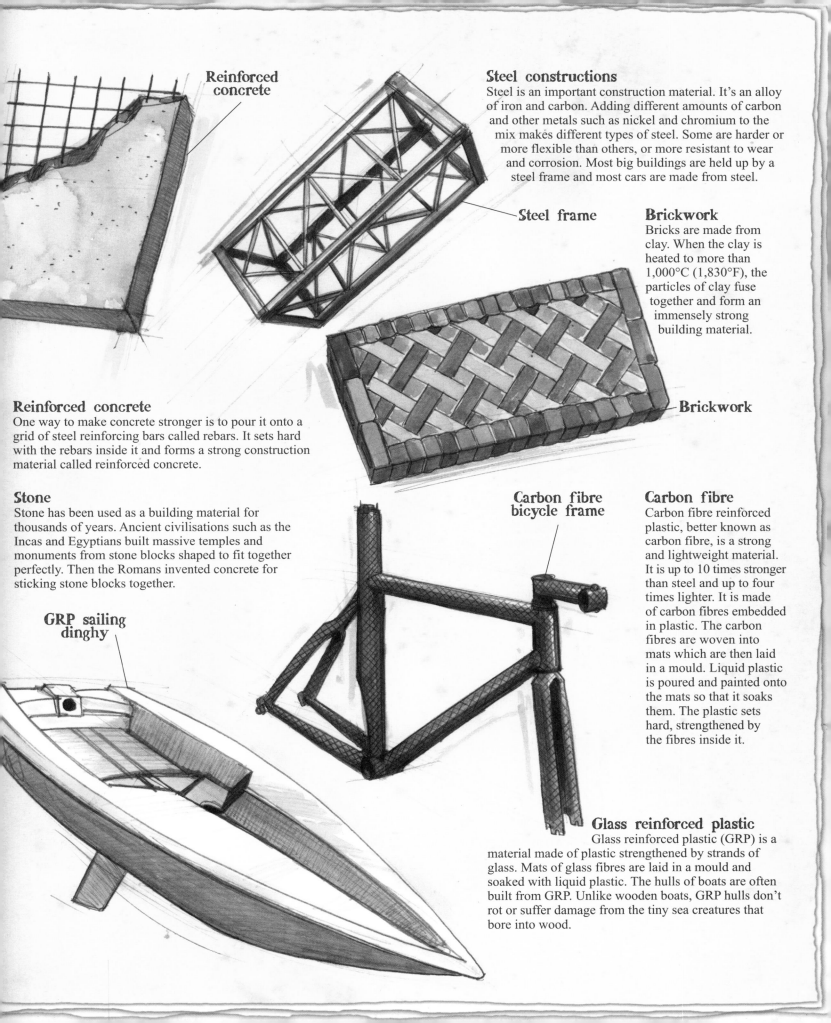

Reinforced concrete

Steel constructions

Steel is an important construction material. It's an alloy of iron and carbon. Adding different amounts of carbon and other metals such as nickel and chromium to the mix makes different types of steel. Some are harder or more flexible than others, or more resistant to wear and corrosion. Most big buildings are held up by a steel frame and most cars are made from steel.

Steel frame

Brickwork

Bricks are made from clay. When the clay is heated to more than 1,000°C (1,830°F), the particles of clay fuse together and form an immensely strong building material.

Brickwork

Reinforced concrete

One way to make concrete stronger is to pour it onto a grid of steel reinforcing bars called rebars. It sets hard with the rebars inside it and forms a strong construction material called reinforced concrete.

Stone

Stone has been used as a building material for thousands of years. Ancient civilisations such as the Incas and Egyptians built massive temples and monuments from stone blocks shaped to fit together perfectly. Then the Romans invented concrete for sticking stone blocks together.

GRP sailing dinghy

Carbon fibre bicycle frame

Carbon fibre

Carbon fibre reinforced plastic, better known as carbon fibre, is a strong and lightweight material. It is up to 10 times stronger than steel and up to four times lighter. It is made of carbon fibres embedded in plastic. The carbon fibres are woven into mats which are then laid in a mould. Liquid plastic is poured and painted onto the mats so that it soaks them. The plastic sets hard, strengthened by the fibres inside it.

Glass reinforced plastic

Glass reinforced plastic (GRP) is a material made of plastic strengthened by strands of glass. Mats of glass fibres are laid in a mould and soaked with liquid plastic. The hulls of boats are often built from GRP. Unlike wooden boats, GRP hulls don't rot or suffer damage from the tiny sea creatures that bore into wood.

treme
risons

Written by
Ian Graham

Illustrated by
Mark Bergin

Created and Designed by
David Salariya

BOOK HOUSE

Contents

IntrOduction

The human race is always trying to outdo itself. Who built the tallest building? Who has travelled furthest into space? Who drove the fastest car and who built it? The answers to some of these questions may change every few years, but when it comes to the highest, biggest and longest, nature has us beaten every time. The tallest man-made structure in the world was only recently completed, but the highest mountain on Earth is already over 10 times bigger!

Throughout the pages of this book you will see for yourself the massive differences in the achievements of man and nature. Compare the fastest horse with the speediest trains, then turn the page to see how the fastest train competes with the fastest aircraft. Prepare your jaw for a drop and your head for a spin, because these extreme comparisons are guaranteed to astound, bewilder and befuddle!

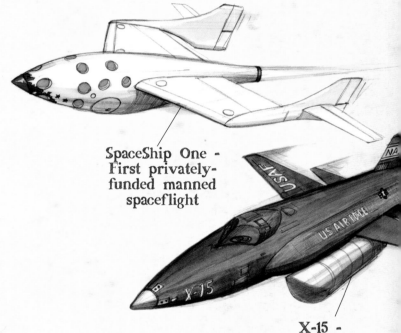

British Westland Lynx - Fastest helicopter: 400 km/h (250 mph)

SpaceShip One - First privately-funded manned spaceflight

X-15 - High altitude: 108 km (67 miles)

Annapurna - Height: 8,091 m (26,545 ft)

Mt McKinley - Height: 6,194 m (20,320 ft)

Nanga Parbat - Height: 8,125 m (26,657 ft)

Manaslu - Height: 8,163 m (26,781 ft)

Aconcagua - Height: 6,960 m (22,834 ft).

MiG-25 Foxbat -
Flew at more than three
times the speed of
sound

Ruppell's Griffon -
Highest recorded
bird in flight:
11,550 m (37,900 ft)

Mercury capsule -
High altitude:
109 km (68 miles)

Spitfire VI -
High altitude:
11,300 m (37,000 ft)

Joseph Kittinger -
Highest balloon ascent:
31,333 m (102,800 ft)

Orville Wright -
First powered
aeroplane flight

Lockheed
SR-71 Blackbird -
Air speed record:
3,529 km/h (2,194 mph)

Piper Warrior -
High speed:
215 km/h (135 mph)

Fastest

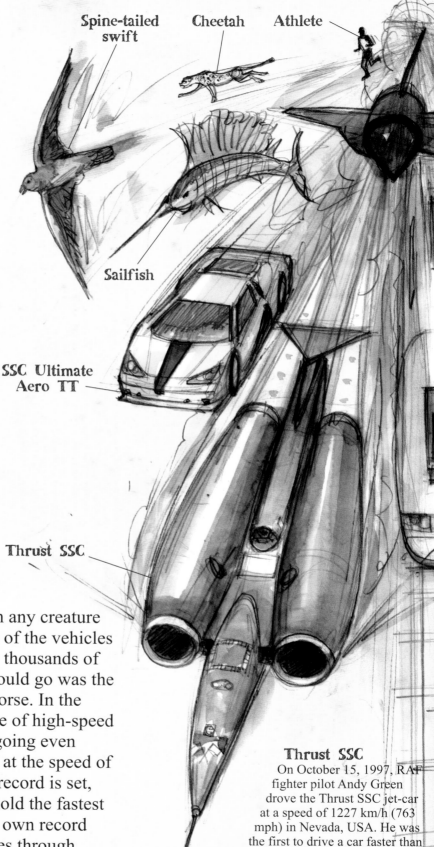

Spine-tailed swift
Cheetah
Athlete
Sailfish
SSC Ultimate Aero TT
Thrust SSC

Athlete

The fastest humans are athletes who can manage speeds of about 35 km/h (21.7 mph) for a few seconds, but they are no match for the fastest animals and vehicles.

Cheetah

The cheetah is the fastest land animal. It's more than three times faster than the best human runner. It can reach a top speed of 120 km/h (75 mph), but only in short bursts of 10-15 seconds at a time.

Bird

A cheetah couldn't catch the world's fastest bird. The spine-tailed swift can reach a speed of 170 km/h (105 mph) in level flight. That's five times faster than the fastest human athlete.

Fish

The sailfish's long slender body slips through water fast. In fact, it's the fastest fish of all, with a speed of up to 110 km/h (68 mph), or about as fast as a cheetah on land.

Production car

The fastest car manufactured for driving on ordinary roads is the SSC Ultimate Aero TT. This American sports car became the new record holder on October 9, 2007, with a speed of 412 km/h (256 mph).

We can go far faster than any creature on Earth with the help of the vehicles we have invented. For thousands of years, the fastest we could go was the speed of a galloping horse. In the 1800s, trains gave people their first experience of high-speed travel, but it wasn't long before people were going even faster. In the 20th century, planes could travel at the speed of a bullet and beyond. Every time a new speed record is set, someone goes even faster. Spacecraft which hold the fastest records today look slow compared to nature's own record breaker, the speed of light. A light beam flashes through space at 300,000 km (186,000 miles) per second.

Thrust SSC

On October 15, 1997, RAF fighter pilot Andy Green drove the Thrust SSC jet-car at a speed of 1227 km/h (763 mph) in Nevada, USA. He was the first to drive a car faster than the speed of sound.

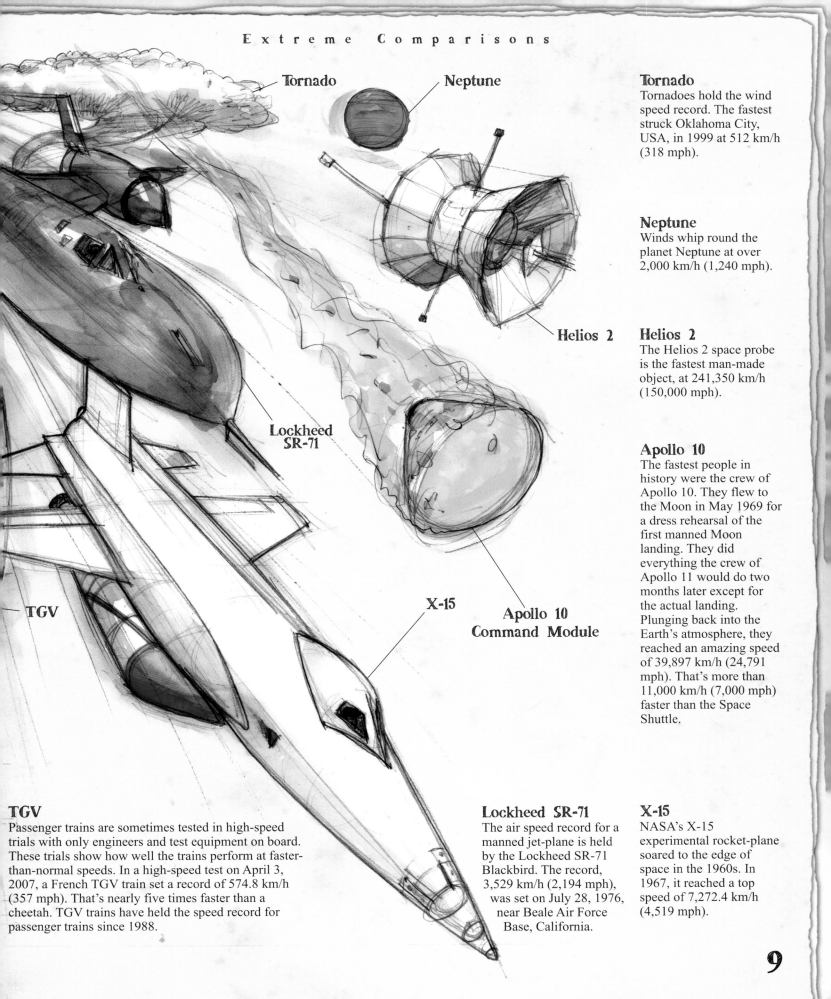

Tornado

Neptune

Helios 2

Lockheed SR-71

X-15

Apollo 10 Command Module

TGV

Tornado
Tornadoes hold the wind speed record. The fastest struck Oklahoma City, USA, in 1999 at 512 km/h (318 mph).

Neptune
Winds whip round the planet Neptune at over 2,000 km/h (1,240 mph).

Helios 2
The Helios 2 space probe is the fastest man-made object, at 241,350 km/h (150,000 mph).

Apollo 10
The fastest people in history were the crew of Apollo 10. They flew to the Moon in May 1969 for a dress rehearsal of the first manned Moon landing. They did everything the crew of Apollo 11 would do two months later except for the actual landing. Plunging back into the Earth's atmosphere, they reached an amazing speed of 39,897 km/h (24,791 mph). That's more than 11,000 km/h (7,000 mph) faster than the Space Shuttle.

TGV
Passenger trains are sometimes tested in high-speed trials with only engineers and test equipment on board. These trials show how well the trains perform at faster-than-normal speeds. In a high-speed test on April 3, 2007, a French TGV train set a record of 574.8 km/h (357 mph). That's nearly five times faster than a cheetah. TGV trains have held the speed record for passenger trains since 1988.

Lockheed SR-71
The air speed record for a manned jet-plane is held by the Lockheed SR-71 Blackbird. The record, 3,529 km/h (2,194 mph), was set on July 28, 1976, near Beale Air Force Base, California.

X-15
NASA's X-15 experimental rocket-plane soared to the edge of space in the 1960s. In 1967, it reached a top speed of 7,272.4 km/h (4,519 mph).

Nature's Speeders

Athlete

The fastest athlete is the holder of the men's 100 metres record. On August 16, 2009, the Jamaican runner Usain Bolt set a world record time of 9.58 seconds at the World Championships in Berlin, Germany. This is equivalent to a speed of around 37 km/h (23 mph).

Galloping racehorse

The fastest horses are American quarter horses. They're specially bred for sprint races over short distances. They have been clocked at 88 km/h (55 mph).

Ostrich

The ostrich is the biggest living bird. It's too heavy to fly, but it has a running speed of 70 km/h (43 mph), faster than any other bird on land.

T-Rex

The terrifying Tyrannosaurus Rex dinosaur may have been able to run at up to about 30 km/h (18 mph).

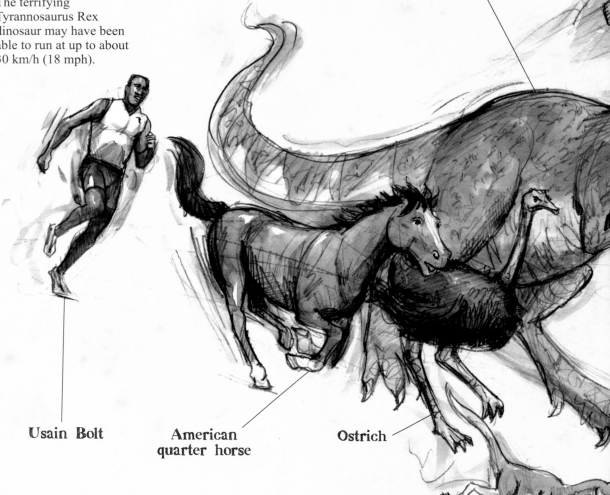

T-Rex

Swimming human

Usain Bolt

American quarter horse

Ostrich

Compsognathus

There is a great range of speeds in the animal kingdom. While sloths hardly seem to move at all, some animals are as fast as a car. A garden snail is one of the slowest, travelling at about 0.05 km/h (0.03 mph). The cheetah is about 2,400 times faster. Even though water is more difficult to move through than air, some creatures can swim faster than a top-class athlete can run. The fastest animals are predators that chase other animals for food. They have to be faster than their prey or they starve, but prey animals are usually fast movers too. A predator can often turn on a short burst of great speed to overcome prey quickly and efficiently.

Fastest dinosaur

The fastest dinosaur of all was probably the Compsognathus. It could run as fast as 65 km/h (40 mph), more than twice as fast as a T-Rex.

Penguin

Penguins can't fly or walk very fast, but they're great swimmers. The gentoo penguin is the fastest of all. Using its wings as fins, it swims underwater at up to 36 km/h (22 mph).

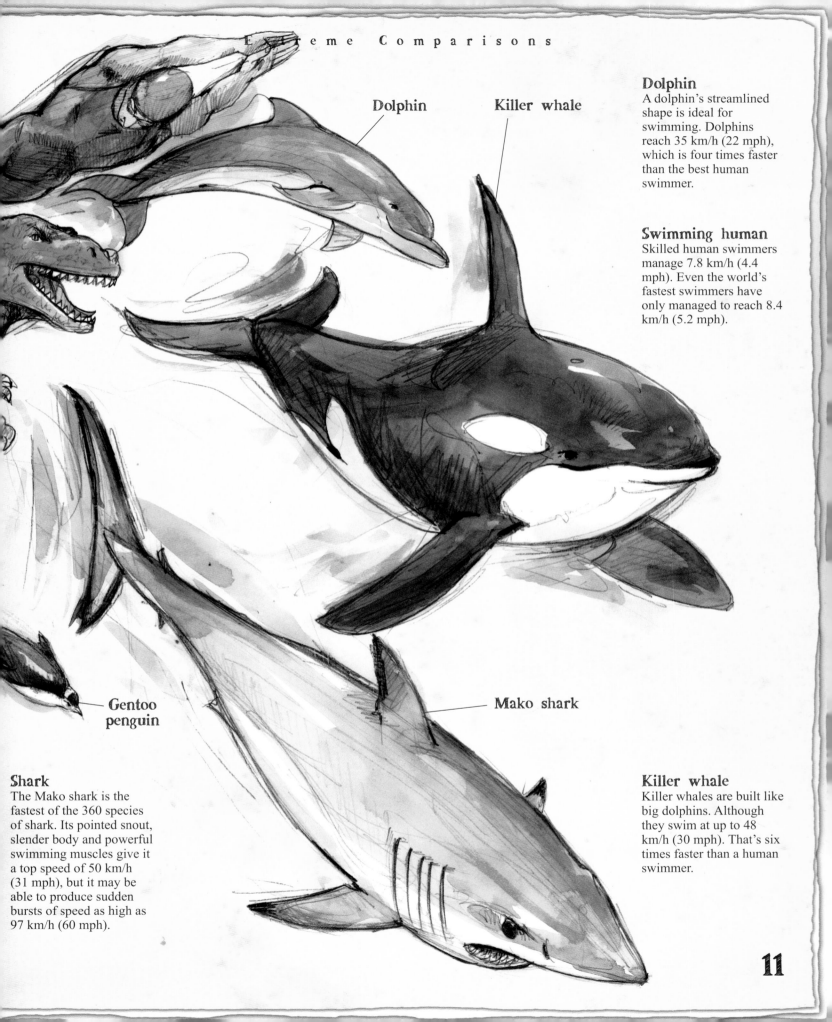

Dolphin

Killer whale

Dolphin
A dolphin's streamlined shape is ideal for swimming. Dolphins reach 35 km/h (22 mph), which is four times faster than the best human swimmer.

Swimming human
Skilled human swimmers manage 7.8 km/h (4.4 mph). Even the world's fastest swimmers have only managed to reach 8.4 km/h (5.2 mph).

Gentoo penguin

Mako shark

Shark
The Mako shark is the fastest of the 360 species of shark. Its pointed snout, slender body and powerful swimming muscles give it a top speed of 50 km/h (31 mph), but it may be able to produce sudden bursts of speed as high as 97 km/h (60 mph).

Killer whale
Killer whales are built like big dolphins. Although they swim at up to 48 km/h (30 mph). That's six times faster than a human swimmer.

11

Trains

High-speed trains whisk passengers from city to city at up to 320 km/h (200 mph). The tracks are made as straight as possible to avoid any loss of speed on bends. These trains are powered by electric motors, using electricity supplied by high-voltage wires above the track.

TGV
TGV trains have been in use in France since 1981. Travelling at up to 320 km/h (200 mph), they go so fast that drivers can't see track-side signals. Instead, the signals appear on the driver's control panel.

ICE
ICE (Inter-City Express) is a German high-speed train. Regular ICE services began in 1991. The trains run at up to 300 km/h (186 mph) on special tracks. A version called ICE-T tilts as it goes round bends.

Transrapid
Transrapid is a German maglev, or magnetic levitation train, which was the first to go into service carrying fare-paying passengers. The first maglev was built in China, to connect the city of Shanghai with its international airport 30 km (19 miles) away. Transrapid passenger services began in 2004. The trains run at 430 km/h (267 mph).

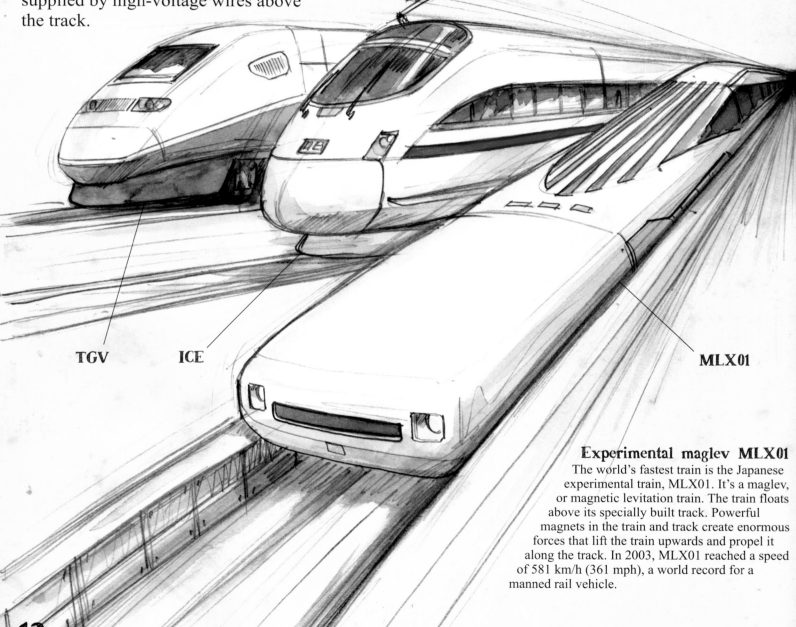

TGV

ICE

MLX01

Experimental maglev MLX01
The world's fastest train is the Japanese experimental train, MLX01. It's a maglev, or magnetic levitation train. The train floats above its specially built track. Powerful magnets in the train and track create enormous forces that lift the train upwards and propel it along the track. In 2003, MLX01 reached a speed of 581 km/h (361 mph), a world record for a manned rail vehicle.

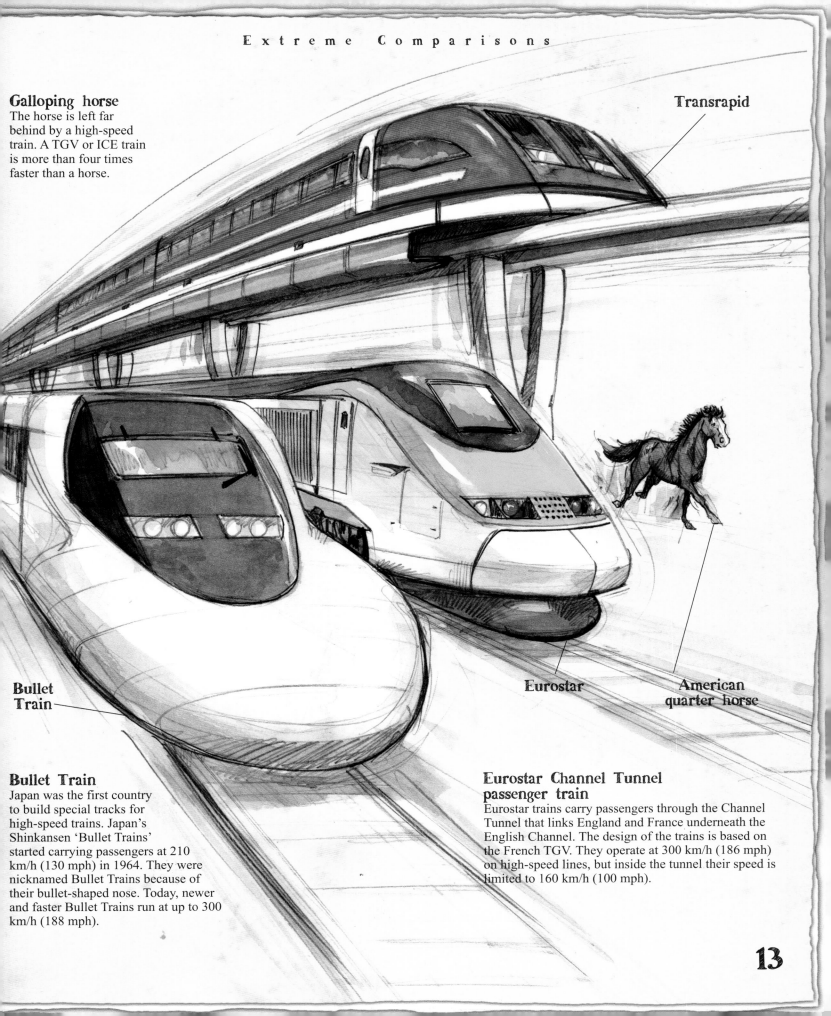

Galloping horse
The horse is left far behind by a high-speed train. A TGV or ICE train is more than four times faster than a horse.

Transrapid

Bullet Train

Eurostar

American quarter horse

Bullet Train
Japan was the first country to build special tracks for high-speed trains. Japan's Shinkansen 'Bullet Trains' started carrying passengers at 210 km/h (130 mph) in 1964. They were nicknamed Bullet Trains because of their bullet-shaped nose. Today, newer and faster Bullet Trains run at up to 300 km/h (188 mph).

Eurostar Channel Tunnel passenger train
Eurostar trains carry passengers through the Channel Tunnel that links England and France underneath the English Channel. The design of the trains is based on the French TGV. They operate at 300 km/h (186 mph) on high-speed lines, but inside the tunnel their speed is limited to 160 km/h (100 mph).

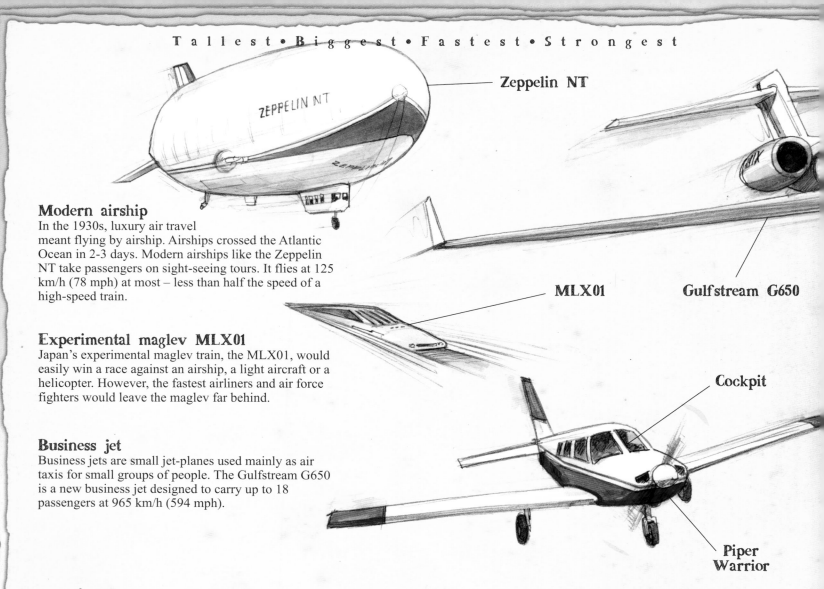

Zeppelin NT

Modern airship

In the 1930s, luxury air travel meant flying by airship. Airships crossed the Atlantic Ocean in 2-3 days. Modern airships like the Zeppelin NT take passengers on sight-seeing tours. It flies at 125 km/h (78 mph) at most – less than half the speed of a high-speed train.

MLX01   **Gulfstream G650**

Experimental maglev MLX01

Japan's experimental maglev train, the MLX01, would easily win a race against an airship, a light aircraft or a helicopter. However, the fastest airliners and air force fighters would leave the maglev far behind.

Cockpit

Business jet

Business jets are small jet-planes used mainly as air taxis for small groups of people. The Gulfstream G650 is a new business jet designed to carry up to 18 passengers at 965 km/h (594 mph).

Piper Warrior

Aircraft

To go faster than a maglev train, passengers have to take to the air. Airliners cruise the skies just under the speed of sound. Supersonic fighters fly faster than the speed of sound. Helicopters are not as fast because of the way they fly. Spinning blades push air downwards and lift a helicopter off the ground. Tilting the blades blows some of the air backwards which propels the helicopter forwards. Although helicopters are not as fast as many other aircraft, their spinning blades enable them to hover motionless in the air and land in small spaces. Their special flying abilities make them ideal for police, air ambulance and rescue work.

Light aircraft

Light aircraft give many people their first taste of piloting a plane. Light aircraft like the Piper Warrior are used for training pilots and also for personal use by pilots. The Warrior flies at up to 215 km/h (135 mph), or just over a third the speed of the fastest maglev train.

Airbus A380

The world's biggest airliner has two passenger decks, one above the other, and space for 853 seats. although most airlines install just over 500. It made its first commercial flight in 2007, from Singapore to Sydney, Australia. It cruises at a speed of about 900 km/h (560 mph), about three times faster than a high-speed train like the French TGV or German ICE train.

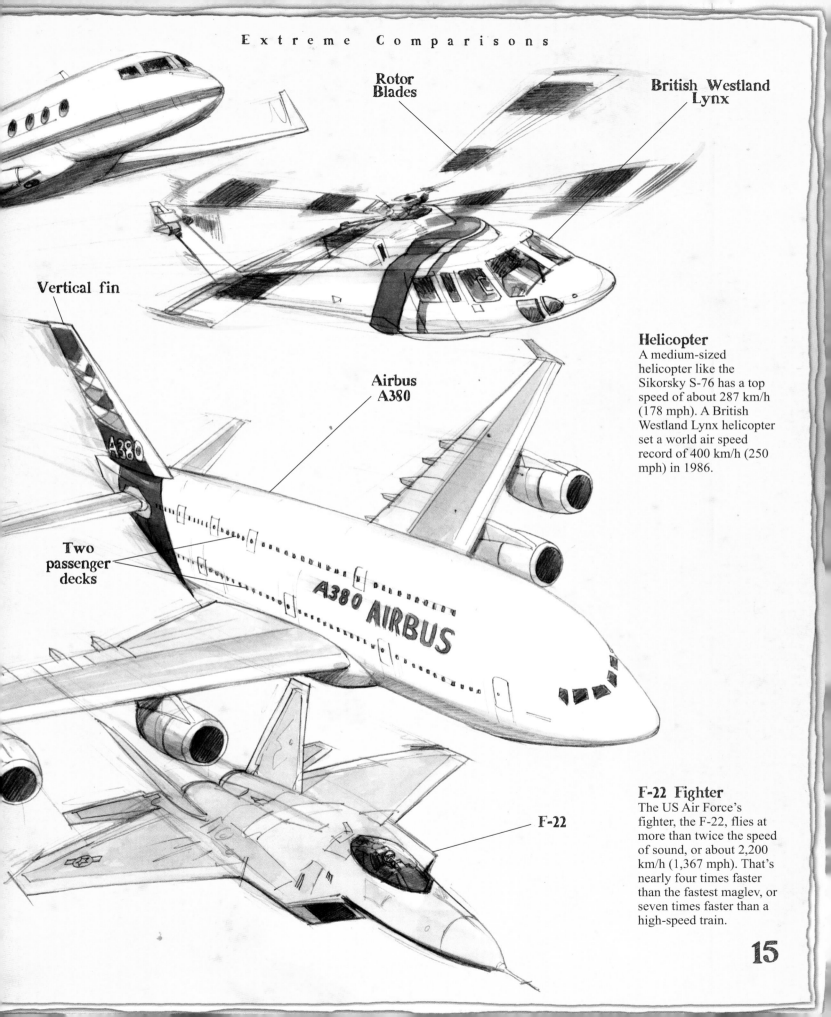

Rotor
Blades

British Westland
Lynx

Vertical fin

Airbus
A380

A380

Two
passenger
decks

A380 AIRBUS

F-22

Helicopter
A medium-sized helicopter like the Sikorsky S-76 has a top speed of about 287 km/h (178 mph). A British Westland Lynx helicopter set a world air speed record of 400 km/h (250 mph) in 1986.

F-22 Fighter
The US Air Force's fighter, the F-22, flies at more than twice the speed of sound, or about 2,200 km/h (1,367 mph). That's nearly four times faster than the fastest maglev, or seven times faster than a high-speed train.

Big gest

Jupiter

Jupiter is the biggest of the solar system's eight planets. It consists mainly of hydrogen and helium, the same gases the Sun is made of. The Earth would fit more than 11 times across Jupiter's diameter of 142,980 km (88,846 miles) and 1,321 Earths would fit inside it.

Antonov An-225 Mriya

The world's biggest plane is the Antonov An-225 Mriya. It was built in 1988 as a transporter for the Soviet space programme. The giant aircraft is 84 m (275.5 ft) long and has a wingspan of 88 m (290 ft).

Jupiter

Boeing Everett Factory

How big is big? There are different ways of measuring the biggest things. Big planes like the Airbus A380 are measured by their size or how many passengers they carry or how much weight they can lift. Big buildings can be measured by the area of land they cover or the volume of space they enclose. Yet huge man-made objects like planes, ships and buildings are tiny specks compared to planet Earth, while Earth itself is dwarfed by the giant gas planets in the outer reaches of the solar system.

Boeing Everett Factory

Boeing didn't have a building big enough to construct the Boeing 747 in, so they built one at Everett, Washington, USA. The main assembly building is the biggest building in the world by volume. It has been expanded several times to fit in new assembly lines for the 767, 777 and 787 airliners. The building has its own rail terminal, where freight trains unload parts from all over the world. Twenty-six cranes hang from the roof which can lift a combined weight of 846 tonnes (nearly 2 million pounds). Finished planes leave the building through one of six huge doors. The building is so enormous that it needs its own fire department, security force, medical centre, electricity supply and water treatment plant. Its biggest waste water pond is big enough to float an ocean-going ship.

Area: 13.3 million cubic metres (472 million cubic feet)

Volume: 16,000 tonnes (33 million pounds)

Crane track length: 50 km (31 miles)

Door size: Height: 25m (81 ft). Width: 91 m (300 ft) to 107 m (350 ft)

Workforce: 25,000

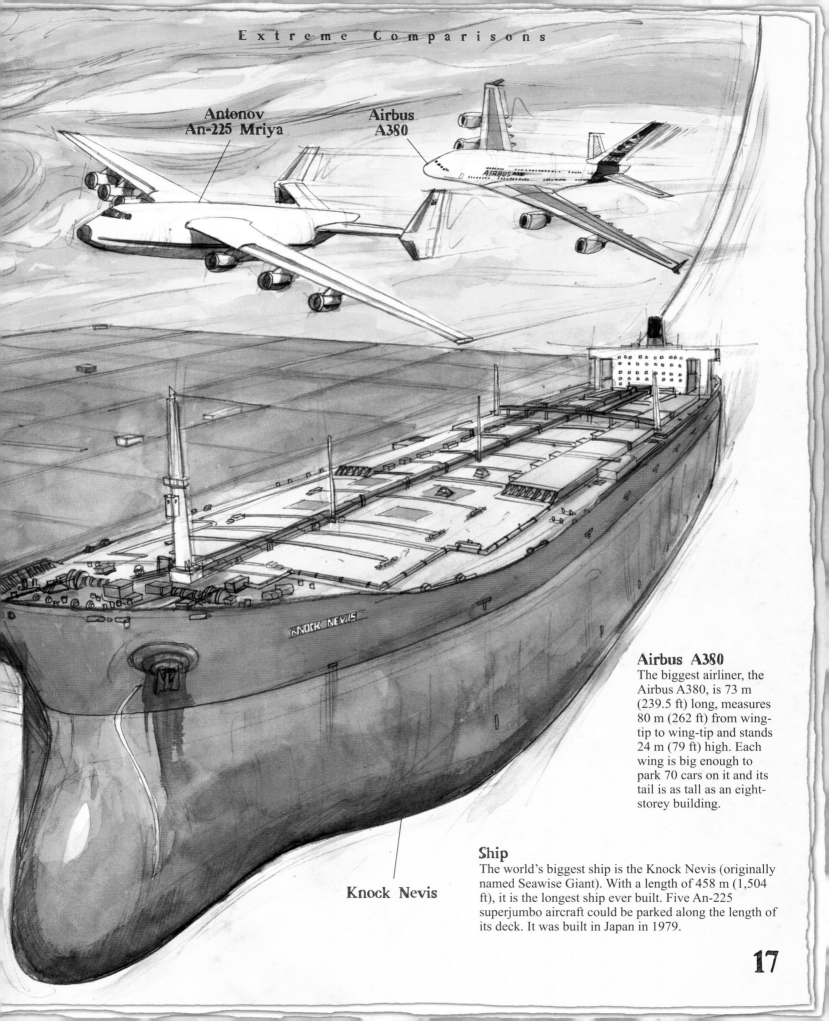

Antonov
An-225 Mriya

Airbus
A380

KNOCK NEVIS

Knock Nevis

Airbus A380
The biggest airliner, the Airbus A380, is 73 m (239.5 ft) long, measures 80 m (262 ft) from wing-tip to wing-tip and stands 24 m (79 ft) high. Each wing is big enough to park 70 cars on it and its tail is as tall as an eight-storey building.

Ship
The world's biggest ship is the Knock Nevis (originally named Seawise Giant). With a length of 458 m (1,504 ft), it is the longest ship ever built. Five An-225 superjumbo aircraft could be parked along the length of its deck. It was built in Japan in 1979.

17

The Great Pyramid at Giza

The Great Pyramid at Giza, Egypt, was built in about 2,560 BC. Its base covers an area of about 53,000 square metres (570,000 square feet).

St Peter's, Rome

St Peter's Basilica in Vatican City, Italy, is one of the world's biggest churches. It covers 23,000 square metres (250,000 square feet) and can fit 60,000.

Stockholm Globe arena

Built in 1989, The Stockholm Globe Arena in Sweden is the world's biggest hemispherical building. The arena is 110 m (361 ft) across, with a seating capacity of 16,000. It is used for music concerts and sports events like ice hockey matches.

Brandenburg airship building

The CargoLifter hangar in Brandenburg, Germany, was constructed in 2000 to house an airship, but the airship was never built. It is 360 m (1,200 ft) long, 210 m (700 ft) wide and 107 m (350 ft) high. It covers an area of 75,600 square metres (814,000 square feet).

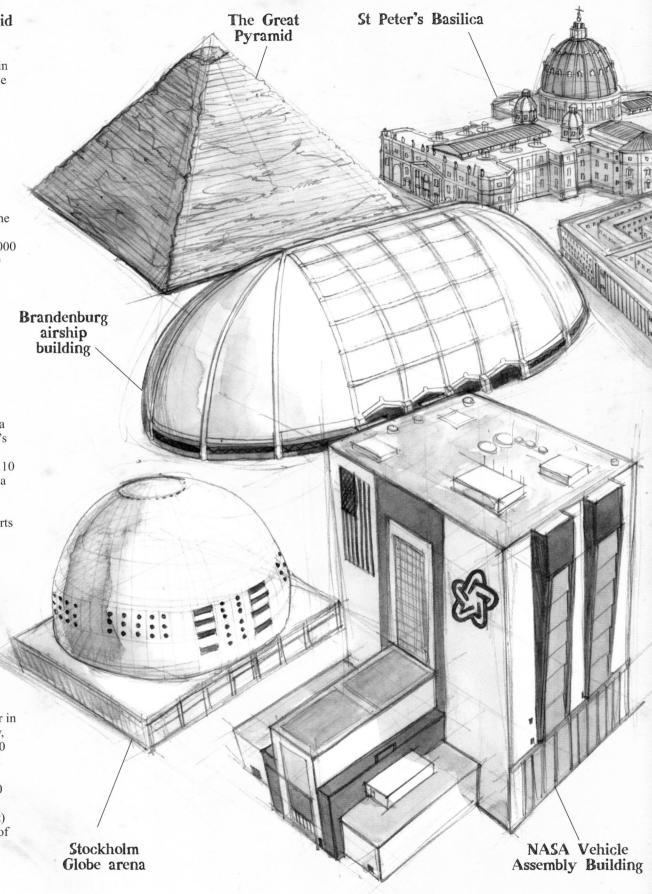

The Great Pyramid

St Peter's Basilica

Brandenburg airship building

Stockholm Globe arena

NASA Vehicle Assembly Building

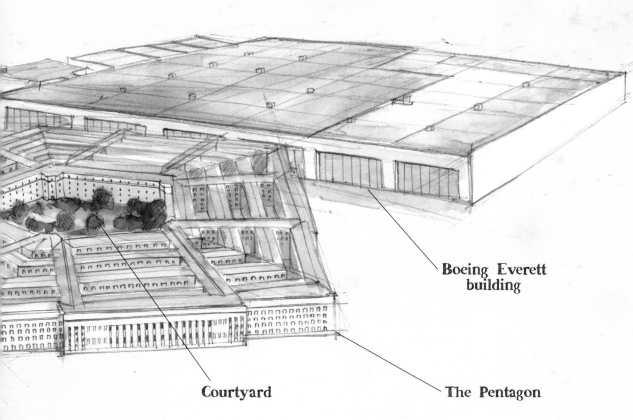

Boeing Everett building

Courtyard

The Pentagon

Big Buildings

Some of the earliest big buildings were tombs. The pyramids of ancient Egypt were built as tombs for the Pharaohs, the rulers of Egypt. The biggest of these, the Great Pyramid, was built to house the body of Pharaoh Khufu. Other big buildings were temples, places of worship, or places where offerings were made to the gods. The biggest buildings of the modern age are built for more practical reasons. Most of them are factories or assembly buildings where giant aircraft or space vehicles are made. Some other buildings are entertainment and sporting venues. These are the domes, stadiums and arenas with enough room inside for huge audiences to sit and watch sport or music concerts. The Colosseum, built in Rome more than 2,000 years ago, is an arena where 50,000 spectators watched games and contests between gladiators. The biggest stadiums today can seat more than 100,000 people, but they're more likely to be watching a far less violent sports event!

Boeing building

Boeing's Everett assembly building in Washington state, USA, covers an area of 398,000 square metres (4.3 million square feet). It's such a huge enclosed area that 50 full-size soccer pitches could be laid out side-by-side. The Boeing assembly building covers the floor area of seven Great Pyramids with enough space left over to fit in St Peter's Basilica too!

The Pentagon

The Pentagon, near Washington DC, USA, is the headquarters of the US Department of Defence. It was built during World War II (1939-45) to bring together the staff of the War Department. The construction work took only 16 months. Today, 23,000 people work in its offices, which cover an area of 344,280 square metres (3,705,800 square feet). The Pentagon has 28.2 km (17.5 miles) of corridors, but it should take no more than seven minutes to walk between any two points in the building.

NASA VAB

NASA's Vehicle Assembly Building (VAB) was built at the Kennedy Space Centre in Florida in 1966. It stands 160 m (525 ft) high and covers an area of 32,375 square metres (350,000 square feet). It is currently used for preparing Space Shuttles for launch, but soon it will be home to new space vehicles that will take astronauts to the Moon and maybe even to Mars.

Rungnado May Day Stadium

Rungnado May Day Stadium

North Korea's Rungnado May Day Stadium is the biggest sports stadium in the world. It was built in 1989. The stadium can hold 150,000 spectators. Its roof reaches a height of over 60 m (197 ft).

Big Buildings: Large & Famous

Louisiana Superdome

Some of the world's biggest buildings and structures stand out from others because of their immense size or their unique, recognisable design. The Bird's Nest stadium's role in the 2008 Olympic Games in Beijing, China, made it the world's most famous sports stadium. The Leaning Tower of Pisa isn't very big or unusual, yet it is one of the most famous towers on Earth because its lean makes it so recognisable.

The Great Pyramid

Pyramid

Egypt's many pyramids are famous for their immense size and great age. Most famous are the three largest pyramids at Giza. The biggest, the Great Pyramid, is the only survivor of the seven wonders of the ancient world.

Sagrada Familia

Sagrada Familia was designed by the Catalan architect, Antoni Gaudí. Construction began in 1882 and is not expected to be finished until about 2026.

Ulm Cathedral

Ulm Cathedral in Germany is the world's tallest church. It measures 162 m (530 ft) to the top of its spire. Construction began in 1377, but it was not finished until 1890. It seats 2,000 people.

Tower of Pisa

The Leaning Tower of Pisa, Italy, started leaning soon after construction began in 1173. It continued leaning until emergency rescue work brought it to a halt in the 1990s.

Statue of Liberty

The Statue of Liberty stands on Liberty Island in New York Harbour. It was gifted by the people of France in 1886. From the ground to the tip of the torch, it measures 93 m (305 ft).

Notre Dame

Notre Dame de Paris is a famous cathedral in Paris. Built in the French Gothic style between 1163 and 1345, it is one of the oldest structures in Paris. It can hold up to 9,000 worshipers.

Sagrada Familia

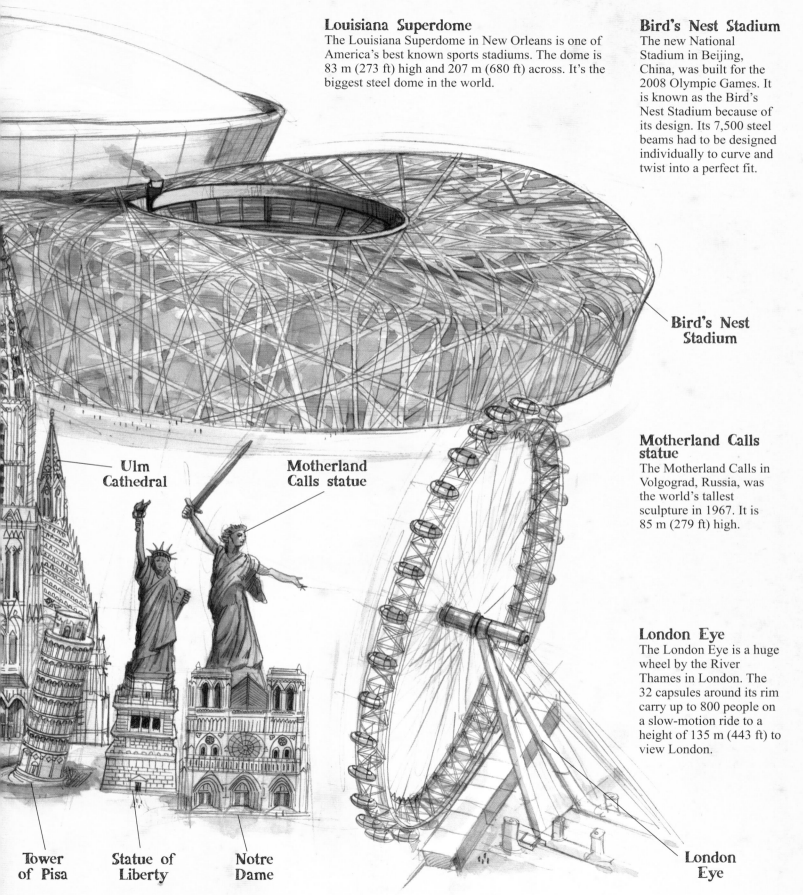

Louisiana Superdome
The Louisiana Superdome in New Orleans is one of America's best known sports stadiums. The dome is 83 m (273 ft) high and 207 m (680 ft) across. It's the biggest steel dome in the world.

Bird's Nest Stadium
The new National Stadium in Beijing, China, was built for the 2008 Olympic Games. It is known as the Bird's Nest Stadium because of its design. Its 7,500 steel beams had to be designed individually to curve and twist into a perfect fit.

Bird's Nest Stadium

Motherland Calls statue
The Motherland Calls in Volgograd, Russia, was the world's tallest sculpture in 1967. It is 85 m (279 ft) high.

Ulm Cathedral

Motherland Calls statue

London Eye
The London Eye is a huge wheel by the River Thames in London. The 32 capsules around its rim carry up to 800 people on a slow-motion ride to a height of 135 m (443 ft) to view London.

Tower of Pisa

Statue of Liberty

Notre Dame

London Eye

21

Tallest Buildings

The skyscrapers that tower above every modern city today can trace their history back to Chicago in 1885. The first skyscraper was Chicago's Home Insurance Building. It had 10 stories. A frame of iron and steel supported the building's weight instead of thick walls. This made it possible to build very tall buildings with thin walls. The skyscraper was made possible by another invention, the safety elevator. Invented by Elisha Otis in 1853, it provided a way of moving people up and down a skyscraper quickly and safely.

1. One World Trade Centre
One World Trade Centre in New York is being built on the site of the World Trade Centre's twin towers, which were destroyed in a terrorist attack on September 11, 2001. It will stand 417 m (1,368 ft) high, and should be completed by 2013.

2. Burj Khalifa
Burj Khalifa is the world's tallest building by a long way. It stands 828 m (2,717 ft) high, nearly double the height of the Empire State Building. It has the fastest elevators in any skyscraper, travelling at 64 km/h (40 mph).

3. Empire State Building
New York's Empire State Building is one of the most famous tall buildings. It was the world's tallest skyscraper for 41 years. In 1931 it was the first building with more than 100 floors. It has 102 floors. It measures 381 m (1,250 ft) to its roof-top, and 449 m (1,472 ft) with its antenna.

4. Jin Mao Tower
In Shanghai, the Jin Mao Building towers 370 m (1,214 ft) above the surrounding streets. A spire on its roof raises its total height to 421 m (1,380 ft).

5. CN Tower
A 553 m (1,815 ft) high communications tower in Toronto, Canada. A restaurant near the top rotates every 72 minutes. The Sky Pod, 447 m (1,465 ft) above the ground, is the world's highest public observation deck.

6. Shanghai World Financial Centre
In 2007, this 492 m (1,615 ft) skyscraper became the tallest structure on the Chinese mainland and the third tallest building in the world. The building has a very distinctive appearance.

7. Sears Tower
This tower in Chicago was the world's tallest building in 1974. TV masts bring its total height to 527 m (1,730 ft). It has 104 elevators and 110 floors. The 103rd floor is an observation deck called the Skydeck.

18. Taipei 101
The second tallest building is 509 m (1,670 ft) tall including a 60 m (197 ft) spire on its roof. It was built in Taipei, Taiwan, in 2004.

17. Petronas Towers
Built in Kuala Lumpur, Malaysia, in 1998, these were the world's tallest buildings until 2004. They are 452 m (1,482 ft) high. An enclosed walkway links the towers at the 41st and 42nd floors.

16. Landmark Tower
Japan's tallest building was completed in Yokohama in 1993. It is 296 m (970 ft) tall.

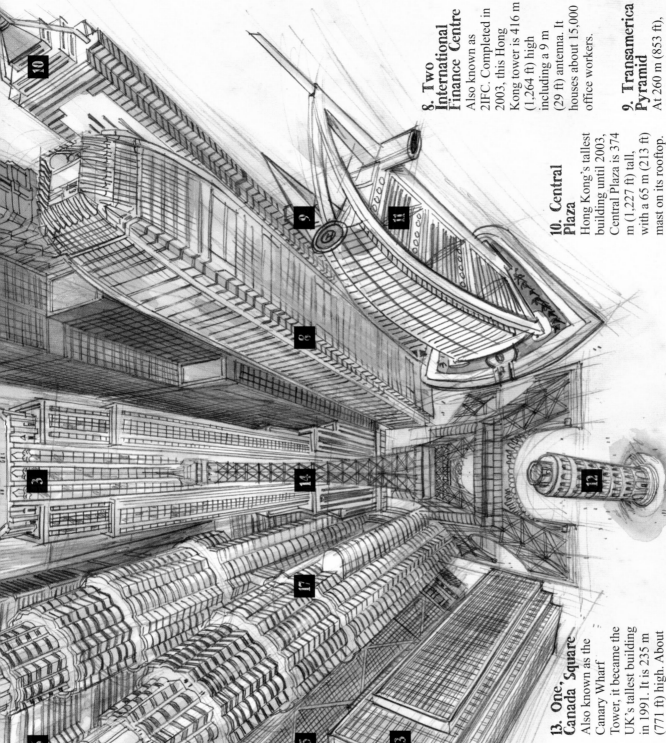

8. Two International Finance Centre
Also known as 2IFC. Completed in 2003, this Hong Kong tower is 416 m (1,264 ft) high including a 9 m (29 ft) antenna. It houses about 15,000 office workers.

9. Transamerica Pyramid
At 260 m (853 ft), this San Francisco building is the tallest in northern California. Its 3,678 windows turn 360 degrees, to enable easy cleaning.

10. Central Plaza
Hong Kong's tallest building until 2003, Central Plaza is 374 m (1,227 ft) tall, with a 65 m (213 ft) mast on its rooftop.

11. Burj al Arab
This hotel in Dubai became the world's tallest hotel when it opened in 1999. It is 321 m (1,053 ft) high. It remained the tallest hotel until 2008, when it was overtaken by the Rose Tower, Dubai. Burj al Arab's design resembles the shape of a boat's sail.

12. Leaning Tower of Pisa
This famous 55 m (183 ft) Italian tower leans because it was built with poor foundations on weak ground.

13. One, Canada Square
Also known as the Canary Wharf Tower, it became the UK's tallest building in 1991. It is 235 m (771 ft) high. About 9,000 people work in the tower. Its structural frame weighs 27,000 tonnes, with a further 47,000 tonnes of stainless steel and glass.

14. Eiffel Tower
Built in Paris in 1889, this was the tallest structure in the world until New York's Chrysler building topped it in 1929. Today, with a 12 m (39 ft) antenna on top, it is 324 m (1,063 ft) high.

15. Bank of China Tower
Completed in Hong Kong in 1990, this tower is 367 m (1,205 ft) high including its two masts.

9. Nanga Parbat
A very dangerous mountain to climb. Height: 8,125 m (26,657 ft) Location: Himalayas.

8. Manaslu
The summit towers above the surrounding ridges and glaciers. Height: 8,163 m (26,781 ft) Location: Himalayas

7. Dhaulagiri
In the Nepalese part of the Himalayas. Height: 8,172 m (26,811 ft). Location: Himalayas

6. Cho Oyu
Found near Mt Everest, on the border between Nepal and China. Height: 8,201 m (26,906 ft) Location: Himalayas

5. Makalu
Found 22 km (14 miles) east of Mt Everest. Height: 8,481 m (27,824 ft). Location: Himalayas

10 Annapurna

9 Nanga Parbat

8 Manaslu

11 Aconcagua

12 Mt McKinley

10. Annapurna
The Annapurna massif is a chain of linked mountains. Height: 8,091 m (26,545 ft) Location: Himalayas

11. Aconcagua
The highest mountain in the western hemisphere. Height: 6,960 m (22,834 ft). Location: South America

12. Mt McKinley
The highest mountain in North America. Height: 6,194 m (20,320 ft). Location: Alaska, North America

13. Kilimanjaro
This dormant volcano is the highest mountain in Africa. Its top is always covered with snow. Height: 5,895 m (19,341 ft). Location: Tanzania, Africa

Mountains

Towering skyscrapers like Burj Khalifa are amazing achievements of modern engineering, but they are dwarfed by nature's own high-rise constructions – mountains. Mt Everest, the world's tallest mountain, is more than 10 times the height of Burj Khalifa. Most mountains were created when the vast moving plates of rock that form the Earth's crust pushed against each other and forced the ground upwards. The Himalayas, home to the world's tallest mountains, were formed by the Indian plate pushing north into the Asian plate. Some mountains are formed by volcanoes. They grow taller as each eruption after eruption piles up layer upon layer of lava.

14. Mt Elbrus
The highest mountain in Europe is a volcano (dormant for 2,000 years). Height: 5,642 m (18,442 ft) Location: Russia

16. Mauna Kea
A volcano which measures 9,800 m (32,000 ft) from the ocean floor – higher than Mt Everest. Height: 4,205 m (13,796 ft) Location: Hawaii

18. Mt Cook
Its native Maori name is Aoraki, meaning 'Cloud Piercer'. Height: 3,754 m (12,316 ft) Location: New Zealand

15. Mont Blanc
The highest mountain in Western Europe stands on the border between Italy and France. Height: 4,810 m (15,781 ft) Location: The Alps

17. Mt Fuji
Japan's highest mountain is an active volcano, although it hasn't erupted since 1707. Height: 3,776 m (12,387 ft) Location: Japan

19. Mt Kosciusko
Named by Polish explorer, Paul Strzelecki, who was the first person to climb it in 1840. Height: 2,228 m (7,310 ft) Location: Australia

4. Lhotse
Connected to Mt Everest by a mountain pass, the South Col. Height: 8,516 m (27,940 ft). Location: Himalayas

3. Kanchenjunga
Straddles the border of India and Nepal. Height: 8,586 m (28,169 ft), Location: Himalayas

2. K2
The world's second highest mountain. Height: 8,611 m (28,251 ft). Location: Himalayas.

1. Mt Everest
The highest point on Earth. Height: 8,848 m (29,028 ft). Location: Himalayas

1 Mt Everest

2 K2

7 Dhaulagiri

6 Cho Oyu

4 Lhotse

5 Makalu

3 Kanchenjunga

13 Kilimanjaro

14 Mt Elbrus

15 Mont Blanc

17 Mt Fuji

18 Mt Cook

16 Mauna Kea

19 Mt Kosciusko

20. Mt Vesuvius
The only volcano on the mainland of Europe to have erupted in the last 100 years. A famous eruption in AD79 destroyed Pompeii. Height: 1,277 m (4,190 ft) Location: Italy

20 Mt Vesuvius

Burj Khalifa

KVLY-TV Tower

Empire State Building

CN Tower

Eiffel Tower

The Great Pyramid

Tallest tree

Sea level

25

Antonov An-225 Mriya

The giant Antonov An-225 Mriya transport plane can weigh up to 600 tonnes (1.3 million pounds), or more than three blue whales.

Ostrich

The heaviest bird alive today is the ostrich, which can weigh up to 156 kg (345 pounds).

Blue whale

The biggest creature that has ever lived on Earth, even bigger than the dinosaurs, is the blue whale. The biggest known blue whale weighed in at 190 tonnes (419,000 pounds).

Engine

Antonov
An-225 Mriya

Kori bustard

The kori bustard and great bustard both qualify as the heaviest bird that can fly. They both weigh up to about 20 kg (44 pounds). The kori bustard is found in Africa, while the great bustard is found across Europe and Asia.

MAN TAKRAF RB293

The heaviest land vehicle is the MAN TAKRAF RB293. It's a bucket wheel excavator and it weighs 13,500 tonnes (29.8 million pounds), or about the same as 70 blue whales.

English Mastiff

The heaviest breed of dog is the English Mastiff. It isn't the biggest dog but it's the heaviest. A large male English Mastiff usually weighs up to about 90 kg (200 pounds). The weight record for the breed is held by a male called Zorba. In 1989, Zorba's weight was recorded as 155 kg (343 pounds).

African elephant

The African male elephant is the heaviest of all land animals. Adult male elephants weigh, on average, about 5.4 tonnes (12,000 pounds), but can be around 7 tonnes (14,430 pounds).

Heaviest

Weights in the natural world vary enormously. The heaviest creature, the blue whale, is 1,200 times heavier than the heaviest bird, the ostrich. The ostrich itself is more than 1,500 times heavier than the heaviest insects. Man-made structures can be many times heavier than the blue whale.

Dromornis stirtoni

The heaviest flightless bird that ever lived was called Dromornis stirtoni, or Stirton's Thunder Bird. It weighed about 500 kg (1,100 pounds). It was more than three times heavier than an ostrich. It lived in Australia more than 6 million years ago.

Kori
bustard

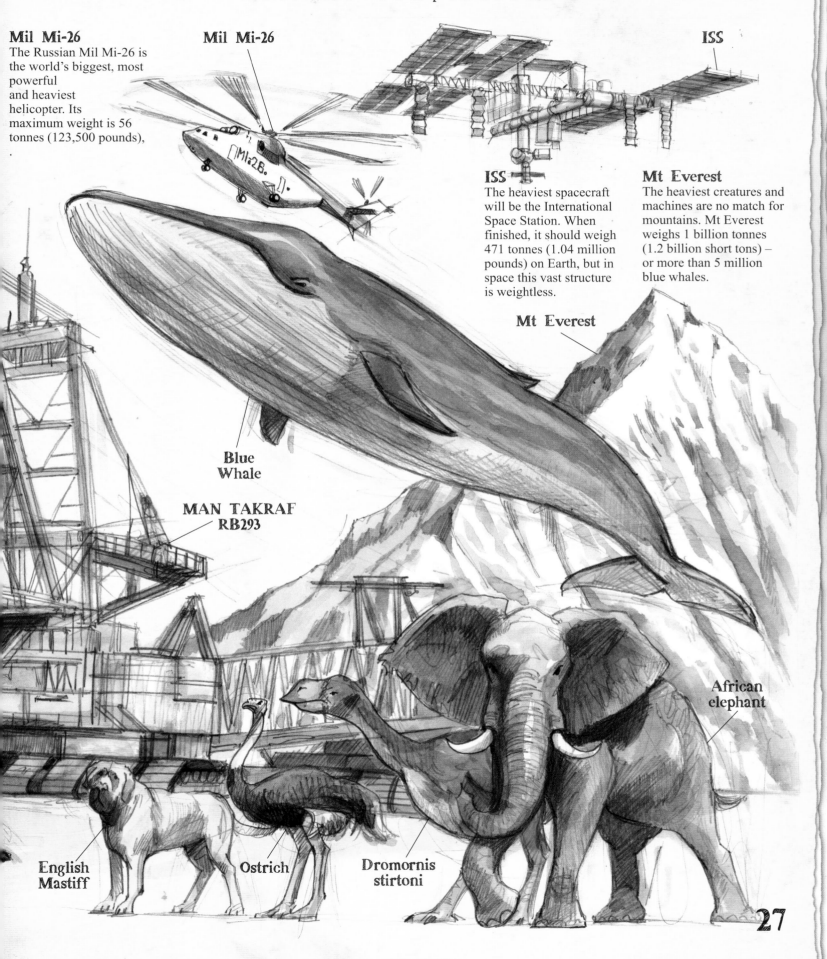

Mil Mi-26
The Russian Mil Mi-26 is the world's biggest, most powerful and heaviest helicopter. Its maximum weight is 56 tonnes (123,500 pounds), .

Mil Mi-26

ISS

ISS
The heaviest spacecraft will be the International Space Station. When finished, it should weigh 471 tonnes (1.04 million pounds) on Earth, but in space this vast structure is weightless.

Mt Everest
The heaviest creatures and machines are no match for mountains. Mt Everest weighs 1 billion tonnes (1.2 billion short tons) – or more than 5 million blue whales.

Mt Everest

Blue Whale

MAN TAKRAF RB293

African elephant

English Mastiff

Ostrich

Dromornis stirtoni

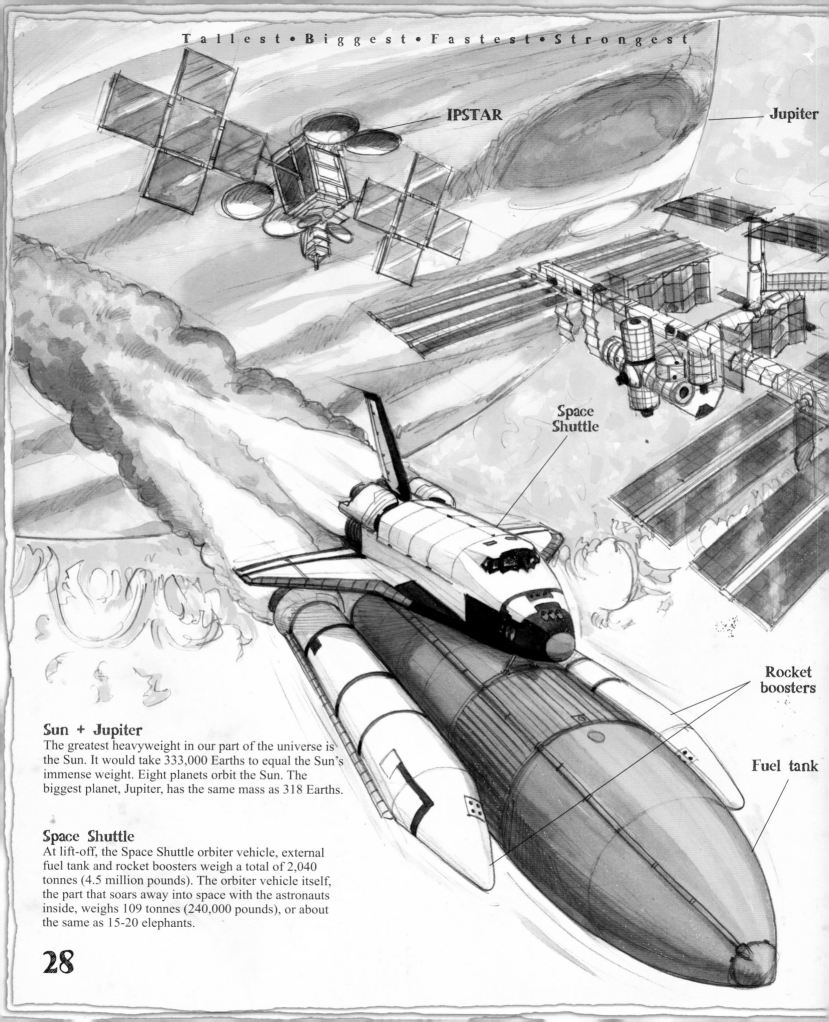

IPSTAR

Jupiter

Space Shuttle

Rocket boosters

Fuel tank

Sun + Jupiter
The greatest heavyweight in our part of the universe is the Sun. It would take 333,000 Earths to equal the Sun's immense weight. Eight planets orbit the Sun. The biggest planet, Jupiter, has the same mass as 318 Earths.

Space Shuttle
At lift-off, the Space Shuttle orbiter vehicle, external fuel tank and rocket boosters weigh a total of 2,040 tonnes (4.5 million pounds). The orbiter vehicle itself, the part that soars away into space with the astronauts inside, weighs 109 tonnes (240,000 pounds), or about the same as 15-20 elephants.

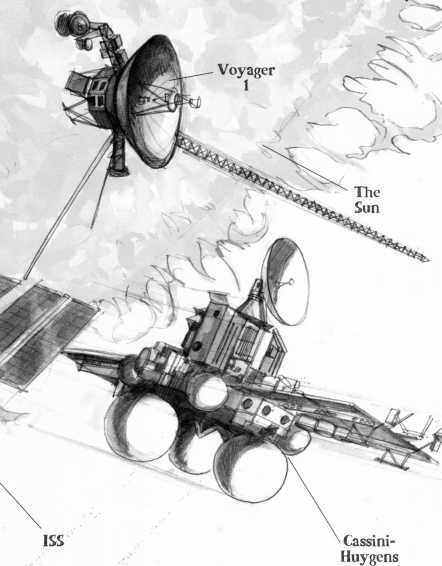

Voyager 1

The Voyager 1 space probe was the first man-made object to leave the solar system. It was launched in 1977 along with Voyager 2. By today's standards, it is quite a lightweight craft. At lift-off, it weighed 772 kg (1,592 pounds).

Cassini-Huygens

The heaviest interplanetary space probe launched by the US space agency, NASA, is Cassini-Huygens. Including a mini-probe called Huygens, the whole craft weighed 2.5 tonnes (5,510 pounds). It was sent on its way to Saturn in 1997 and went into orbit around the ringed planet in 2004.

ISS

The International Space Station is by far the heaviest man-made object ever constructed in space. At 471 tonnes (1 million pounds), it's heavier than four Space Shuttle orbiters or about 95 elephants. Too big for one country to build, 16 nations are working together to provide the ISS with parts and launch vehicles.

IPSTAR

Many of the heaviest satellites launched today are communications satellites. The heaviest is Thaicom-4, also known as IPSTAR-1. It was launched on August 11, 2005, by an Airane-5 rocket to relay broadband Internet signals. The massive satellite weighs 6,486 kg (14,300 pounds), or about as heavy as a large African elephant.

Heavyweights in Space

The first man-made object sent into space was the Soviet satellite, Sputnik 1. Launched on October 4, 1957, Sputnik 1 was a metal ball 58.5 cm (23 in) across with a radio transmitter inside. It weighed just 83.6 kg (184 pounds). Today, the weight of the biggest satellites is measured in tonnes. These space cargoes are launched by rockets. Satellites and spacecraft are bigger and heavier today than in the 1950s, because there are now more powerful rockets to launch them. The biggest and heaviest man-made object in space today is the International Space Station, which is scheduled for completion in 2011. The stars and planets, however, are far more massive than any spacecraft.

Furthest From the Sun

Voyager 1

Neptune

Jupiter

Jupiter

On its voyage through the solar system and beyond, Voyager 1 flew past the giant planet Jupiter. The photographs and measurements made by Voyager 1 and its sister craft, Voyager 2, taught scientists more about the furthest planets than they had ever learned in the entire history of astronomy.

The Voyager 1 space probe has flown far beyond the solar system's most distant planet, Neptune. It is now leaving the solar system and heading for the stars. Beyond the solar system, the distances between the stars are so immense that kilometres, or even billions of kilometres, are of no use to measure them. These enormous distances are measured in light years. A light year is the distance light travels in one year – roughly 10 trillion kilometres (6 trillion miles). The nearest star, proxima centauri, is 4.3 light years away. All the stars in the sky travel through space together in a vast rotating disc of 200 billion stars called a galaxy. Our galaxy is called the Milky Way. It is so big that a light beam travelling at 300,000 kilometres per second would take 100,000 years to cross it from one side to the other. Wherever astronomers look, they see more and more galaxies. There are billions of them.

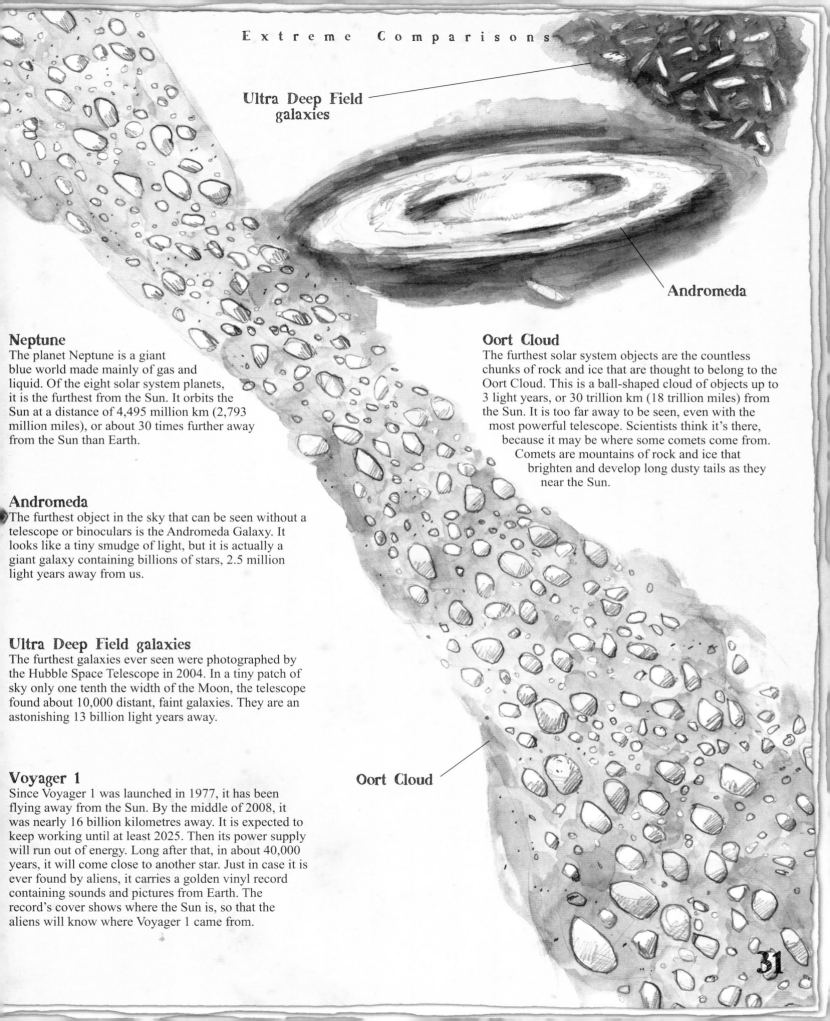

Ultra Deep Field
galaxies

Andromeda

Neptune

The planet Neptune is a giant blue world made mainly of gas and liquid. Of the eight solar system planets, it is the furthest from the Sun. It orbits the Sun at a distance of 4,495 million km (2,793 million miles), or about 30 times further away from the Sun than Earth.

Andromeda

The furthest object in the sky that can be seen without a telescope or binoculars is the Andromeda Galaxy. It looks like a tiny smudge of light, but it is actually a giant galaxy containing billions of stars, 2.5 million light years away from us.

Ultra Deep Field galaxies

The furthest galaxies ever seen were photographed by the Hubble Space Telescope in 2004. In a tiny patch of sky only one tenth the width of the Moon, the telescope found about 10,000 distant, faint galaxies. They are an astonishing 13 billion light years away.

Voyager 1

Since Voyager 1 was launched in 1977, it has been flying away from the Sun. By the middle of 2008, it was nearly 16 billion kilometres away. It is expected to keep working until at least 2025. Then its power supply will run out of energy. Long after that, in about 40,000 years, it will come close to another star. Just in case it is ever found by aliens, it carries a golden vinyl record containing sounds and pictures from Earth. The record's cover shows where the Sun is, so that the aliens will know where Voyager 1 came from.

Oort Cloud

The furthest solar system objects are the countless chunks of rock and ice that are thought to belong to the Oort Cloud. This is a ball-shaped cloud of objects up to 3 light years, or 30 trillion km (18 trillion miles) from the Sun. It is too far away to be seen, even with the most powerful telescope. Scientists think it's there, because it may be where some comets come from. Comets are mountains of rock and ice that brighten and develop long dusty tails as they near the Sun.

Oort Cloud

Great Distances

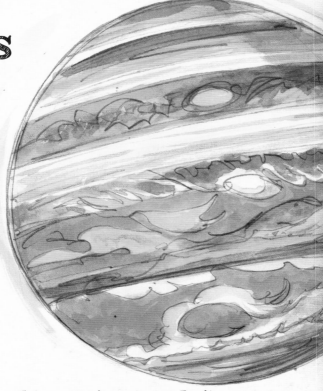

Our home in the vast expanse of the universe is the solar system. It's the Sun and everything that travels through space with it. There are eight planets, several dwarf planets, more than 150 moons and countless smaller objects including comets and asteroids. The solar system extends over a region of space 15 trillion km (9 trillion miles) across. The distances between the planets are so great that spacecraft take years to reach the furthest. Only robot probes have made these journeys so far, but astronauts may take their first steps on another planet, Mars, later this century.

Solar prominence

Mars

Earth and Moon

Venus

Mercury

The Sun

Solar prominence
Fierce magnetic forces on the Sun hurl vast tongues of glowing gas, called solar prominences, into space. These prominences measure up to the width of 40 Earths.

Jupiter
The giant planet Jupiter is 778 million kilometres (483 million miles) from the Sun. It looks like a bright star, but through a telescope its striped clouds and some of its 63 moons can be seen.

Mercury and Venus
Mercury orbits only 58 million kilometres (36 million miles) from the Sun. Venus is nearly twice as far away, 108 million kilometres (67 million miles).

Earth and Moon
Earth and its solitary Moon orbit the Sun at an average distance of 150 million kilometres (93 million miles), also called 1 Astronomical Unit (AU).

Mars
Mars, the red planet, orbits 228 million kilometres (142 million miles) away from the Sun. From Earth, it looks like a small red star.

The Sun
The Sun sits at the centre of the solar system. Its powerful pull of gravity holds the planets in their orbits and stops them drifting off into space. Even the giant Jupiter is held in the Sun's mighty grip.

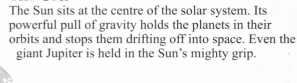

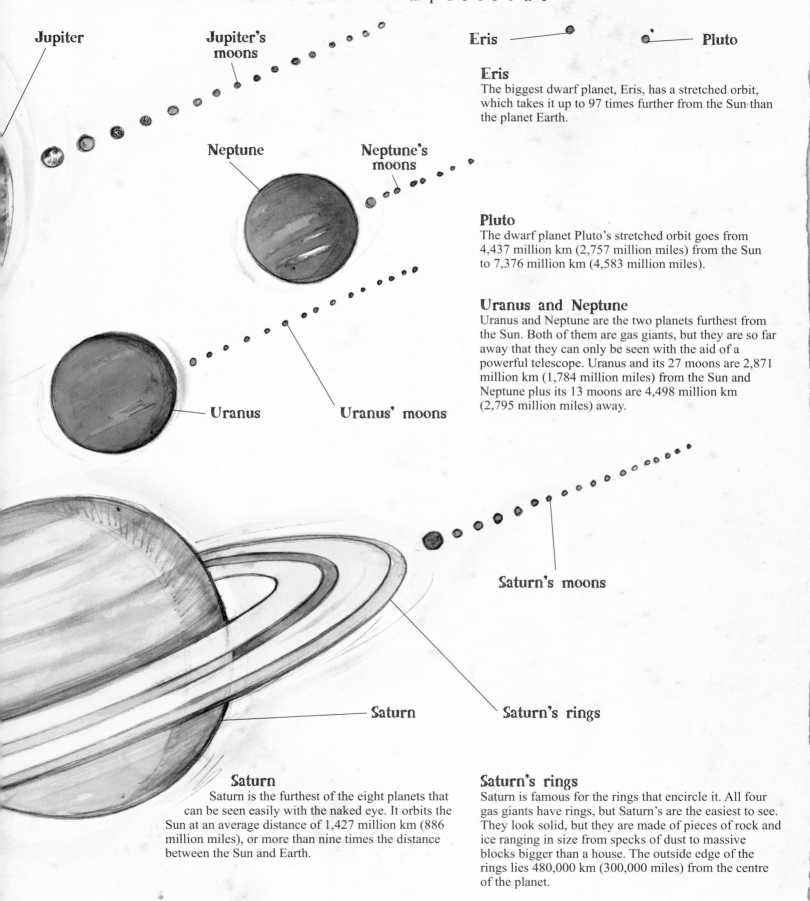

Jupiter

Jupiter's moons

Eris

Pluto

Eris
The biggest dwarf planet, Eris, has a stretched orbit, which takes it up to 97 times further from the Sun than the planet Earth.

Neptune

Neptune's moons

Pluto
The dwarf planet Pluto's stretched orbit goes from 4,437 million km (2,757 million miles) from the Sun to 7,376 million km (4,583 million miles).

Uranus and Neptune
Uranus and Neptune are the two planets furthest from the Sun. Both of them are gas giants, but they are so far away that they can only be seen with the aid of a powerful telescope. Uranus and its 27 moons are 2,871 million km (1,784 million miles) from the Sun and Neptune plus its 13 moons are 4,498 million km (2,795 million miles) away.

Uranus

Uranus' moons

Saturn's moons

Saturn

Saturn's rings

Saturn
Saturn is the furthest of the eight planets that can be seen easily with the naked eye. It orbits the Sun at an average distance of 1,427 million km (886 million miles), or more than nine times the distance between the Sun and Earth.

Saturn's rings
Saturn is famous for the rings that encircle it. All four gas giants have rings, but Saturn's are the easiest to see. They look solid, but they are made of pieces of rock and ice ranging in size from specks of dust to massive blocks bigger than a house. The outside edge of the rings lies 480,000 km (300,000 miles) from the centre of the planet.

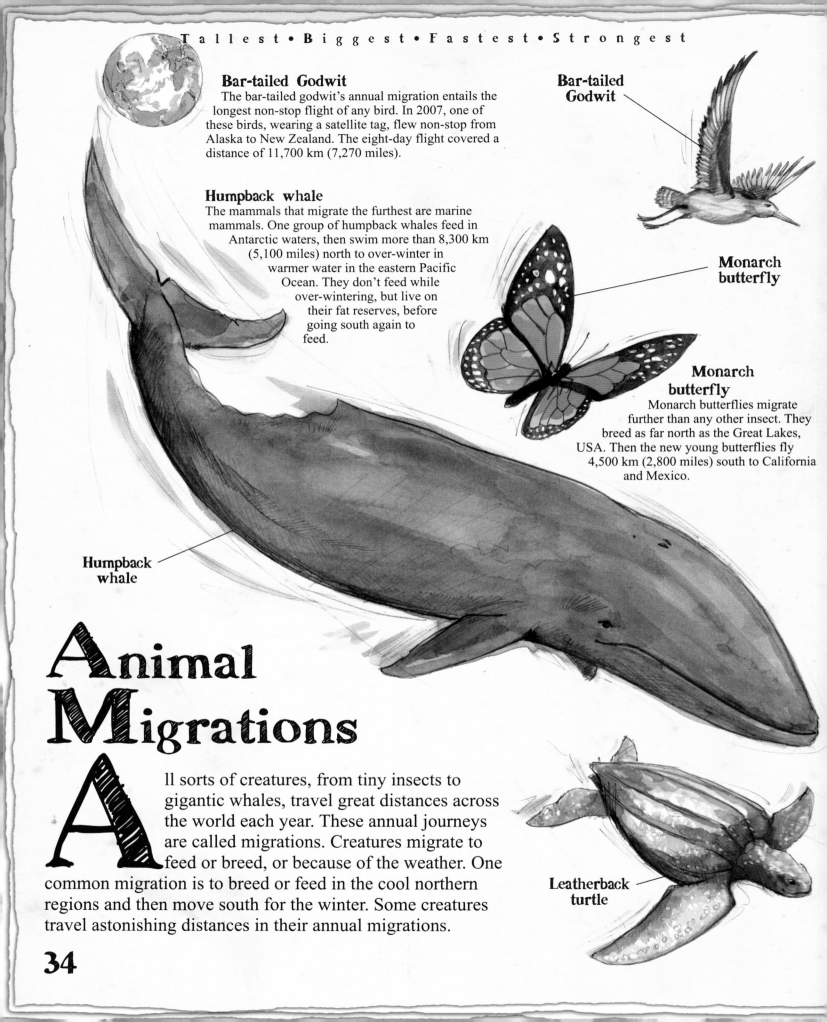

Bar-tailed Godwit

The bar-tailed godwit's annual migration entails the longest non-stop flight of any bird. In 2007, one of these birds, wearing a satellite tag, flew non-stop from Alaska to New Zealand. The eight-day flight covered a distance of 11,700 km (7,270 miles).

Humpback whale

The mammals that migrate the furthest are marine mammals. One group of humpback whales feed in Antarctic waters, then swim more than 8,300 km (5,100 miles) north to over-winter in warmer water in the eastern Pacific Ocean. They don't feed while over-wintering, but live on their fat reserves, before going south again to feed.

Bar-tailed Godwit

Monarch butterfly

Monarch butterfly

Monarch butterflies migrate further than any other insect. They breed as far north as the Great Lakes, USA. Then the new young butterflies fly 4,500 km (2,800 miles) south to California and Mexico.

Humpback whale

Animal Migrations

All sorts of creatures, from tiny insects to gigantic whales, travel great distances across the world each year. These annual journeys are called migrations. Creatures migrate to feed or breed, or because of the weather. One common migration is to breed or feed in the cool northern regions and then move south for the winter. Some creatures travel astonishing distances in their annual migrations.

Leatherback turtle

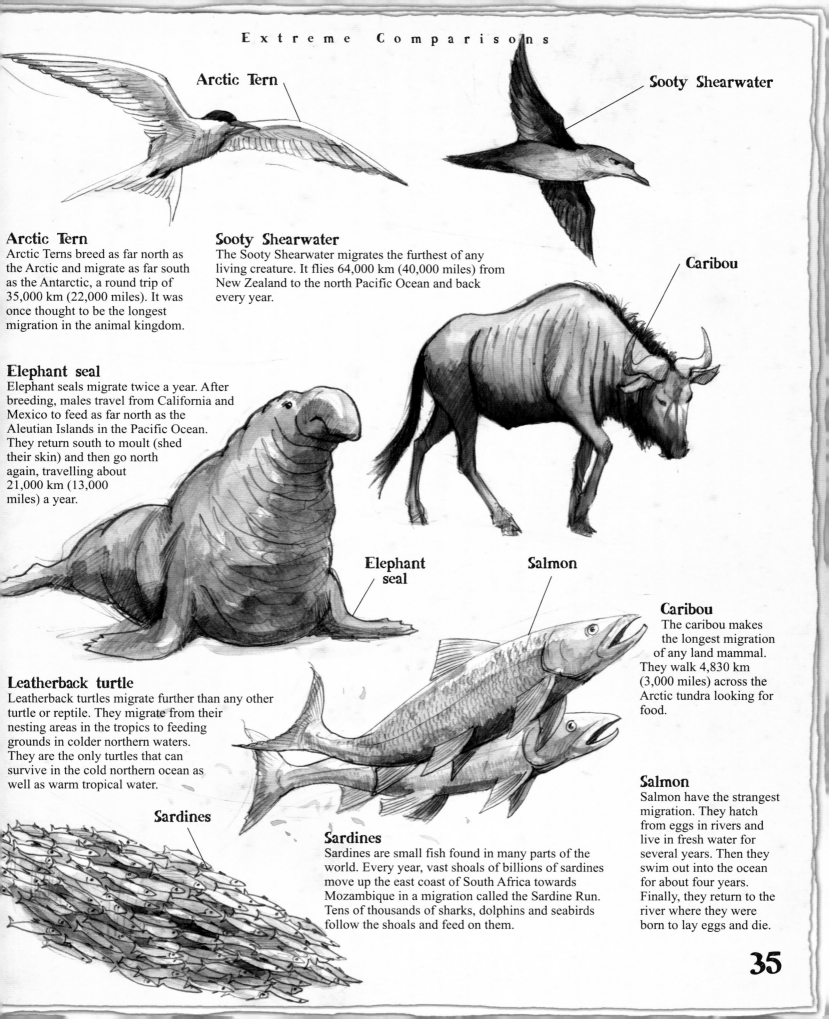

Arctic Tern

Arctic Tern
Arctic Terns breed as far north as the Arctic and migrate as far south as the Antarctic, a round trip of 35,000 km (22,000 miles). It was once thought to be the longest migration in the animal kingdom.

Sooty Shearwater

Sooty Shearwater
The Sooty Shearwater migrates the furthest of any living creature. It flies 64,000 km (40,000 miles) from New Zealand to the north Pacific Ocean and back every year.

Caribou

Elephant seal
Elephant seals migrate twice a year. After breeding, males travel from California and Mexico to feed as far north as the Aleutian Islands in the Pacific Ocean. They return south to moult (shed their skin) and then go north again, travelling about 21,000 km (13,000 miles) a year.

Elephant seal

Salmon

Caribou
The caribou makes the longest migration of any land mammal. They walk 4,830 km (3,000 miles) across the Arctic tundra looking for food.

Leatherback turtle
Leatherback turtles migrate further than any other turtle or reptile. They migrate from their nesting areas in the tropics to feeding grounds in colder northern waters. They are the only turtles that can survive in the cold northern ocean as well as warm tropical water.

Sardines

Sardines
Sardines are small fish found in many parts of the world. Every year, vast shoals of billions of sardines move up the east coast of South Africa towards Mozambique in a migration called the Sardine Run. Tens of thousands of sharks, dolphins and seabirds follow the shoals and feed on them.

Salmon
Salmon have the strangest migration. They hatch from eggs in rivers and live in fresh water for several years. Then they swim out into the ocean for about four years. Finally, they return to the river where they were born to lay eggs and die.

35

Deepest

The mighty Amazon river is up to 40 m (131 ft) deep in the rainy season, but it looks like a puddle compared to the deepest parts of the world's oceans. Challenger Deep in the Mariana Trench, the deepest part of the Pacific Ocean, is more than 270 times deeper than the Amazon River. Exploring the ocean depths is very difficult because of the crushing pressure of the water. Only a handful of craft, manned and unmanned, have gone much deeper than 305 m (1,000 ft).

SCUBA diver
SCUBA divers usually venture no deeper than about 45 m (150 ft), but the record depth for SCUBA diving is 313 m (1,027 ft), using special breathing gases.

SCUBA diver

Free diver
In June, 2007, Herbert Nitsch set a new record of 214 m (700 ft) for diving without any breathing equipment. The record was set in Spetses, Greece.

Free diver

SSN nuclear submarine
Most nuclear submarines are designed to dive to about 305 m (1,000 ft). They must not go deeper or they risk being crushed by the water pressure.

SSN

Hardsuit diver
On August 1, 2006, Chief US Navy Diver Daniel P. Jackson made a record-breaking dive to 610 m (2,000 ft) in an armoured diving suit called a hardsuit.

Hardsuit diver

ALFA sub
The Soviet Project 705 Lira class submarine, known as ALFA in the West, was one of the deepest diving military submarines. They could dive to about 800 m (2,600 ft), but may have been tested to a depth of 1,300 m (4,265 ft).

ALFA submarine

Great white shark
Great White Sharks often patrol shallow coastal waters, but have also been found in the deep ocean down to 1,875 m (6,150 ft).

Great white shark

Sperm whale
The sperm whale, the biggest of all the toothed whales, can dive to depths of around 1,150 m (3,773 ft) and stay there for more than an hour.

Sperm whale

Alvin submersible
A submersible craft called Alvin can dive to a depth of 4,500 m (14,764 ft). It dives with a small robot called Jason Junior.

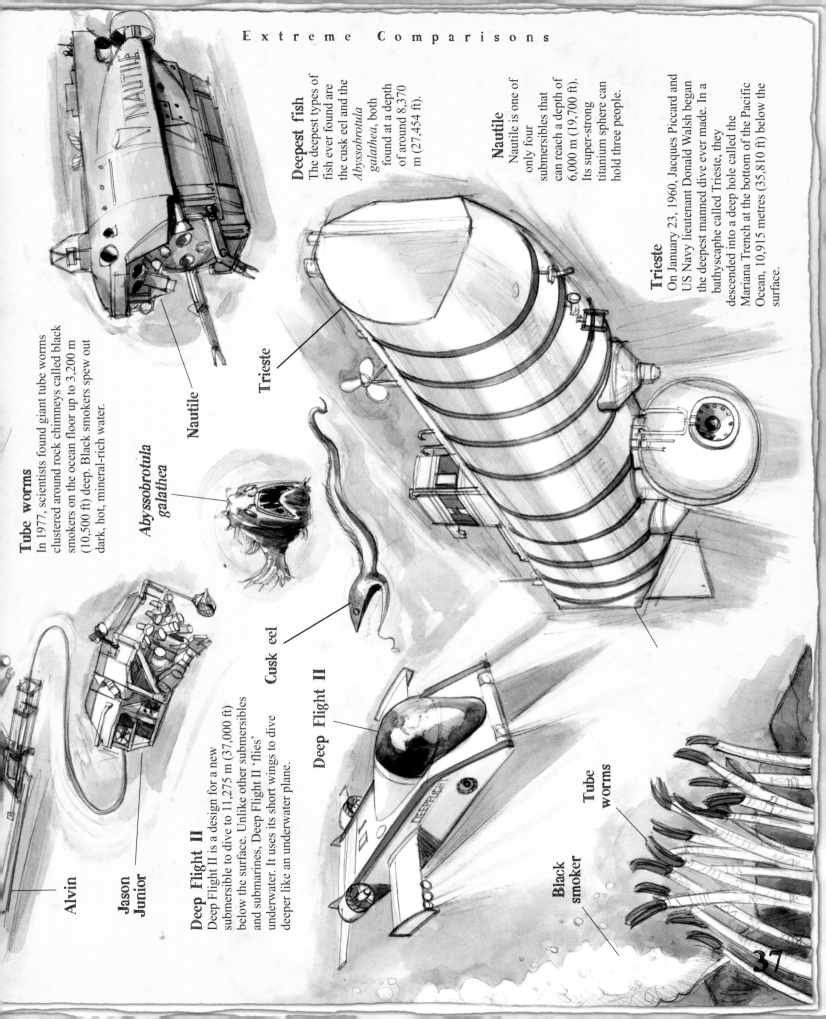

Deepest fish
The deepest types of fish ever found are the cusk eel and the *Abyssobrotula galathea*, both found at a depth of around 8,370 m (27,454 ft).

Nautile
Nautile is one of only four submersibles that can reach a depth of 6,000 m (19,700 ft). Its super-strong titanium sphere can hold three people.

Trieste
On January 23, 1960, Jacques Piccard and US Navy lieutenant Donald Walsh began the deepest manned dive ever made. In a bathyscaphe called Trieste, they descended into a deep hole called the Mariana Trench at the bottom of the Pacific Ocean, 10,915 metres (35,810 ft) below the surface.

Trieste

Nautile

Tube worms
In 1977, scientists found giant tube worms clustered around rock chimneys called black smokers on the ocean floor up to 3,200 m (10,500 ft) deep. Black smokers spew out dark, hot, mineral-rich water.

Abyssobrotula galathea

Cusk eel

Deep Flight II

Tube worms

Black smoker

Deep Flight II
Deep Flight II is a design for a new submersible to dive to 11,275 m (37,000 ft) below the surface. Unlike other submersibles and submarines, Deep Flight II 'flies' underwater. It uses its short wings to dive deeper like an underwater plane.

Alvin

Jason Junior

37

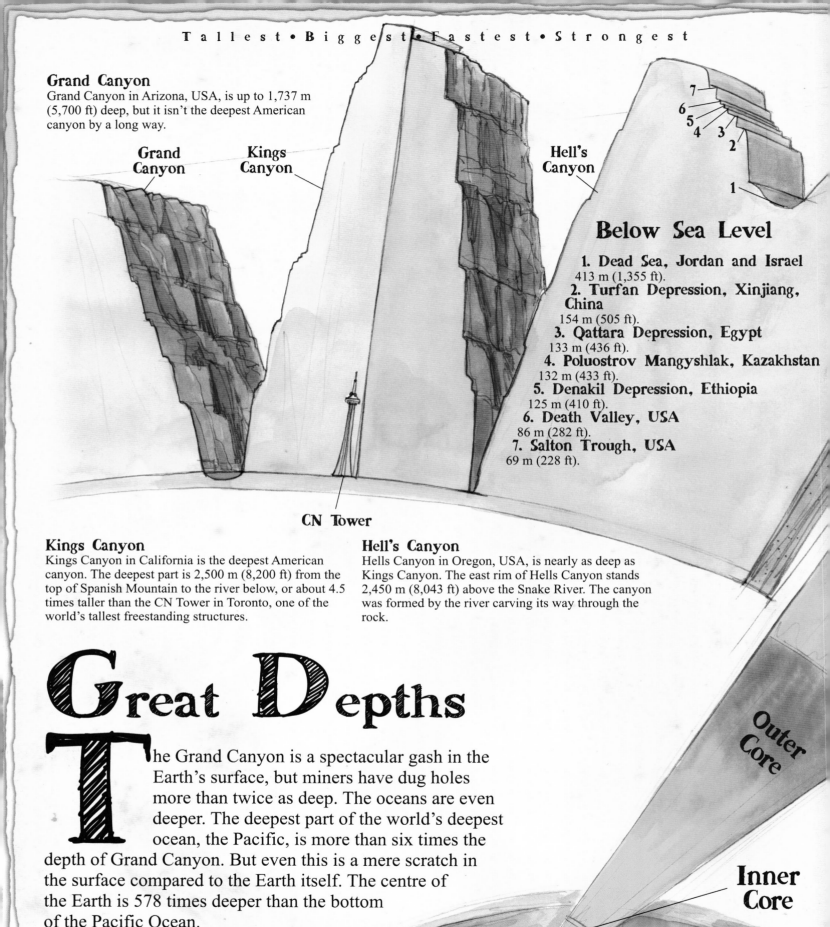

Grand Canyon
Grand Canyon in Arizona, USA, is up to 1,737 m (5,700 ft) deep, but it isn't the deepest American canyon by a long way.

Grand Canyon

Kings Canyon

Hell's Canyon

Below Sea Level

1. Dead Sea, Jordan and Israel
413 m (1,355 ft).
2. Turfan Depression, Xinjiang, China
154 m (505 ft).
3. Qattara Depression, Egypt
133 m (436 ft).
4. Poluostrov Mangyshlak, Kazakhstan
132 m (433 ft).
5. Denakil Depression, Ethiopia
125 m (410 ft).
6. Death Valley, USA
86 m (282 ft).
7. Salton Trough, USA
69 m (228 ft).

CN Tower

Kings Canyon
Kings Canyon in California is the deepest American canyon. The deepest part is 2,500 m (8,200 ft) from the top of Spanish Mountain to the river below, or about 4.5 times taller than the CN Tower in Toronto, one of the world's tallest freestanding structures.

Hell's Canyon
Hells Canyon in Oregon, USA, is nearly as deep as Kings Canyon. The east rim of Hells Canyon stands 2,450 m (8,043 ft) above the Snake River. The canyon was formed by the river carving its way through the rock.

Great Depths

The Grand Canyon is a spectacular gash in the Earth's surface, but miners have dug holes more than twice as deep. The oceans are even deeper. The deepest part of the world's deepest ocean, the Pacific, is more than six times the depth of Grand Canyon. But even this is a mere scratch in the surface compared to the Earth itself. The centre of the Earth is 578 times deeper than the bottom of the Pacific Ocean.

Outer Core

Inner Core

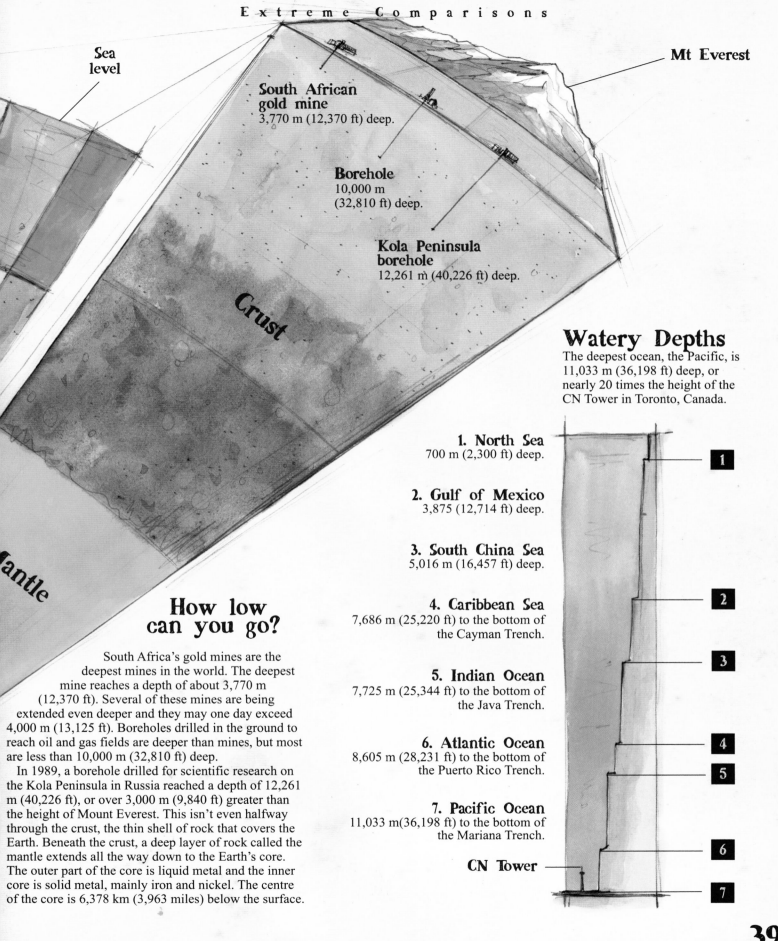

Sea level

South African gold mine
3,770 m (12,370 ft) deep.

Borehole
10,000 m
(32,810 ft) deep.

Kola Peninsula borehole
12,261 m (40,226 ft) deep.

Crust

Mantle

Mt Everest

Watery Depths

The deepest ocean, the Pacific, is 11,033 m (36,198 ft) deep, or nearly 20 times the height of the CN Tower in Toronto, Canada.

1. North Sea
700 m (2,300 ft) deep.

2. Gulf of Mexico
3,875 (12,714 ft) deep.

3. South China Sea
5,016 m (16,457 ft) deep.

4. Caribbean Sea
7,686 m (25,220 ft) to the bottom of the Cayman Trench.

5. Indian Ocean
7,725 m (25,344 ft) to the bottom of the Java Trench.

6. Atlantic Ocean
8,605 m (28,231 ft) to the bottom of the Puerto Rico Trench.

7. Pacific Ocean
11,033 m(36,198 ft) to the bottom of the Mariana Trench.

CN Tower

How low can you go?

South Africa's gold mines are the deepest mines in the world. The deepest mine reaches a depth of about 3,770 m (12,370 ft). Several of these mines are being extended even deeper and they may one day exceed 4,000 m (13,125 ft). Boreholes drilled in the ground to reach oil and gas fields are deeper than mines, but most are less than 10,000 m (32,810 ft) deep.

In 1989, a borehole drilled for scientific research on the Kola Peninsula in Russia reached a depth of 12,261 m (40,226 ft), or over 3,000 m (9,840 ft) greater than the height of Mount Everest. This isn't even halfway through the crust, the thin shell of rock that covers the Earth. Beneath the crust, a deep layer of rock called the mantle extends all the way down to the Earth's core. The outer part of the core is liquid metal and the inner core is solid metal, mainly iron and nickel. The centre of the core is 6,378 km (3,963 miles) below the surface.

39

SpaceShipOne

SpaceShipOne is the spaceplane that made the first privately funded manned spaceflight on June 21, 2004. Mike Melvill was at the controls. Then it won the $10 million Ansari X-Prize by making two further spaceflights within two weeks of one another. Mike Melvill made the first flight on September 29, 2004, and Brian Binnie piloted it for the second flight on October 4 in the same year. All three flights exceeded a height of 100 km (328,000 ft), where space is considered to begin.

SpaceShipOne

X-15

Lockheed SR-71 Blackbird

The Lockheed SR-71 Blackbird spy-plane was one of the highest-flying aircraft ever built. It could cruise at an altitude of 25,900 m (85,000 ft).

X-15

The X-15 research aircraft set an altitude record of 108 km (67 miles) on August 22, 1963. The X-15 was built by North American Aviation for high-altitude, high-speed flight research. Neil Armstrong, the first man to walk on the Moon, was one of the X-15's pilots. The X-15 didn't take off like an ordinary plane. It was launched in the air from beneath the wing of a B-52 bomber. Then the X-15 pilot fired his rocket engine and soared away.

Highest

Airliners cruise the skies as high above sea level as the bottom of the Pacific Ocean is below sea level. Some aircraft are designed to go a lot higher than this. They go higher to carry out research, point cameras at the ground, set altitude records and occasionally win prizes. The first people to probe the upper atmosphere were balloon pilots, who made pioneering high-altitude flights in the 1800s. They quickly discovered that the air high above the ground is too thin to breathe and freezing cold. Some balloon pilots ventured too high and died. Today, high altitude balloon crews travel inside sealed, pressurised capsules that protect them from extreme cold and the shortage of oxygen. The highest that any manned aircraft has flown is 112 km (69.6 miles), or 10 times higher than a normal airliner. It was achieved by the rocket-powered SpaceShipOne on October 4, 2004. The Lockheed SR-71 Blackbird holds the record for manned jet-planes at 25,929 m (85,069 ft).

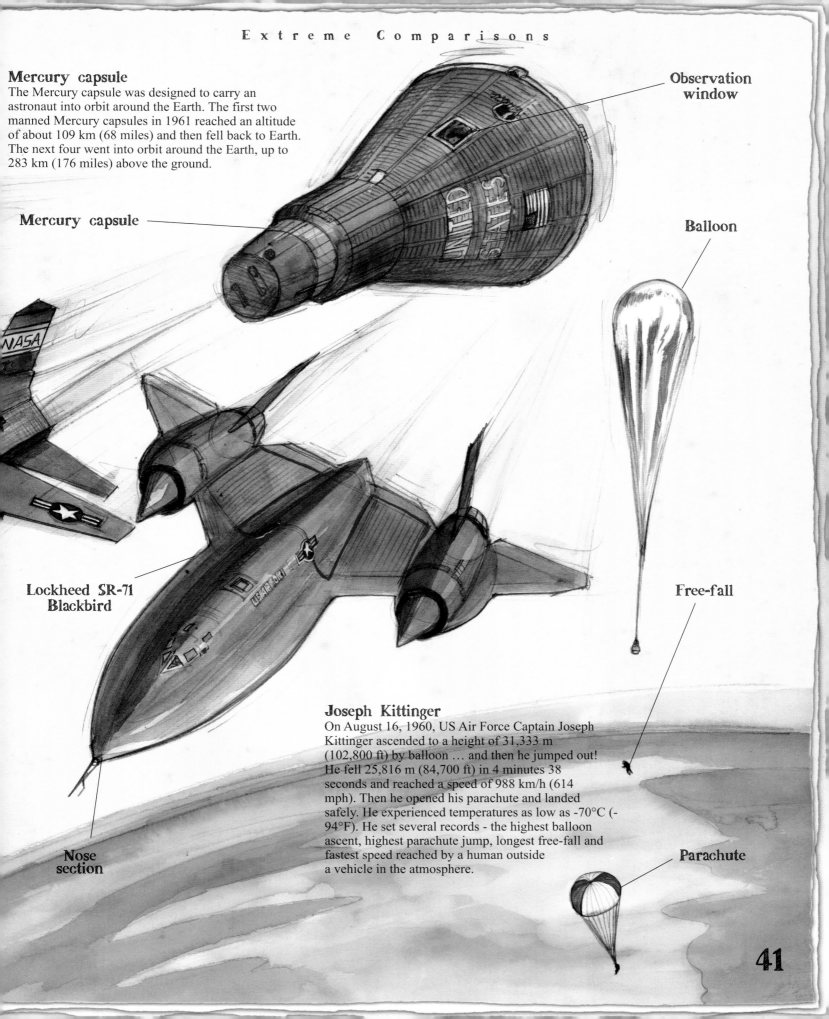

Mercury capsule

The Mercury capsule was designed to carry an astronaut into orbit around the Earth. The first two manned Mercury capsules in 1961 reached an altitude of about 109 km (68 miles) and then fell back to Earth. The next four went into orbit around the Earth, up to 283 km (176 miles) above the ground.

Observation window

Mercury capsule

Balloon

Lockheed SR-71 Blackbird

Free-fall

Joseph Kittinger

On August 16, 1960, US Air Force Captain Joseph Kittinger ascended to a height of 31,333 m (102,800 ft) by balloon … and then he jumped out! He fell 25,816 m (84,700 ft) in 4 minutes 38 seconds and reached a speed of 988 km/h (614 mph). Then he opened his parachute and landed safely. He experienced temperatures as low as -70°C (-94°F). He set several records - the highest balloon ascent, highest parachute jump, longest free-fall and fastest speed reached by a human outside a vehicle in the atmosphere.

Nose section

Parachute

41

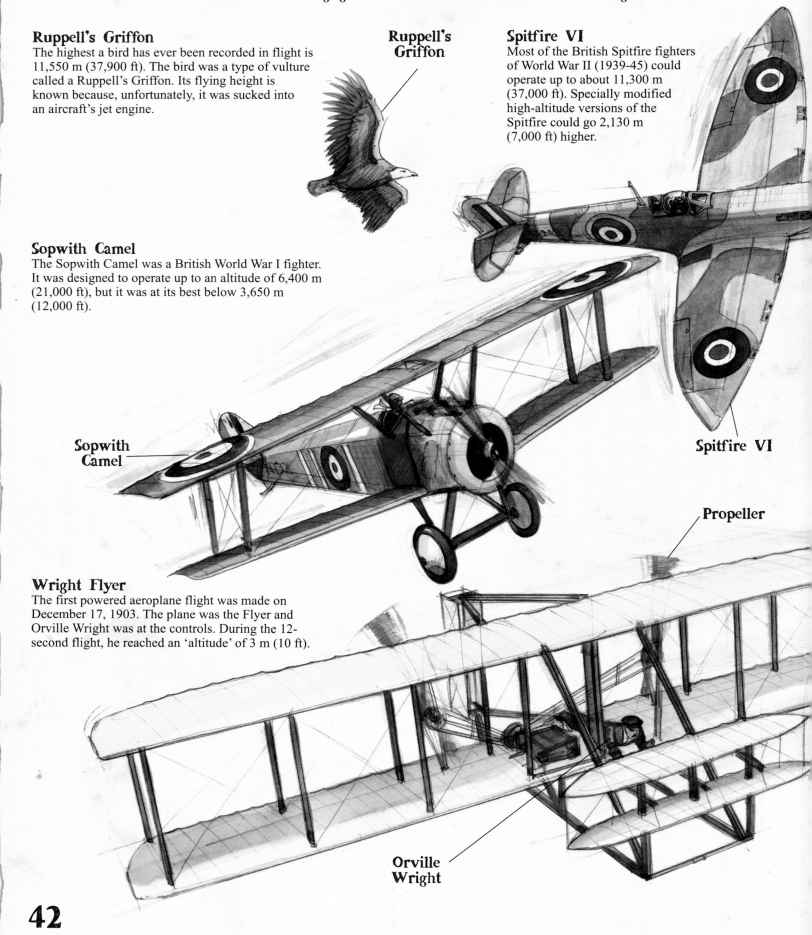

Ruppell's Griffon
The highest a bird has ever been recorded in flight is 11,550 m (37,900 ft). The bird was a type of vulture called a Ruppell's Griffon. Its flying height is known because, unfortunately, it was sucked into an aircraft's jet engine.

Ruppell's Griffon

Spitfire VI
Most of the British Spitfire fighters of World War II (1939-45) could operate up to about 11,300 m (37,000 ft). Specially modified high-altitude versions of the Spitfire could go 2,130 m (7,000 ft) higher.

Sopwith Camel
The Sopwith Camel was a British World War I fighter. It was designed to operate up to an altitude of 6,400 m (21,000 ft), but it was at its best below 3,650 m (12,000 ft).

Sopwith Camel

Spitfire VI

Propeller

Wright Flyer
The first powered aeroplane flight was made on December 17, 1903. The plane was the Flyer and Orville Wright was at the controls. During the 12-second flight, he reached an 'altitude' of 3 m (10 ft).

Orville Wright

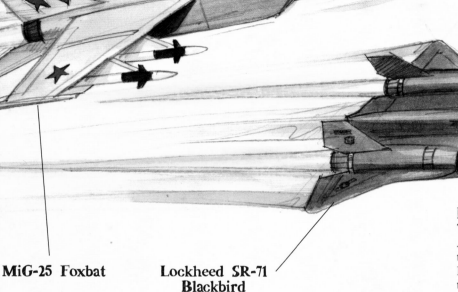

MiG-25 Foxbat
The MiG-25 is a 1970s Russian fighter designed to fly at more than three times the speed of sound. Most MiG-25s had a maximum altitude of about 24,400 m (80,000 ft), but a modified MiG-25 set an altitude record of 37,650 m (123,524 ft) in 1977.

Lockheed SR-71 Blackbird
The Lockheed SR-71 Blackbird was a remarkable American spy-plane built in the 1960s and flown until the 1990s. Its service ceiling was kept a secret, but this Mach 3 (three times the speed of sound) plane is thought to have been able to fly higher than 25,900 m (85,000 ft) to evade enemy fighters.

MiG-25 Foxbat

Lockheed SR-71 Blackbird

Wright Flyer

High Fliers

The maximum altitude at which an aircraft can fly safely is its service ceiling. Military aircraft generally have higher service ceilings than commercial airliners. During World War I (1914-18), fighters and bombers had ceilings of up to about 7,000 m (23,000 ft). By the 1940s, the highest flying planes could reach 12,200 m (40,000 ft). The extra power generated by jet engines enabled planes to go faster and higher. By the 1950s, some military aircraft could exceed 17,000 m (55,775 ft). Today, airliners like the Boeing 777 and Airbus A380 have service ceilings of about 13,000 m (42,650 ft). Bombers can go higher than airliners. The US Air Force B-2 bomber's service ceiling is 15,000 m (50,000 ft). Fighters can fly even higher. The latest US fighter, the F-22 Raptor, can reach 19,810 m (65,000 ft), or almost three times the maximum altitude of a World War I fighter. Spy-planes are the highest flying military planes. The Lockheed U-2 spy-plane can exceed 25,910 m (85,000 ft).

1 **Wright Flyer**
107 yrs old

8 **Oldest rock**
4.28 billion yrs old

1. Oldest flying machine

The Wright brothers' Flyer is the oldest successful aeroplane. Its first flight on December 17, 1903, marked the beginning of modern aviation. Flyer never flew again after that day. Today, it is on display in the Smithsonian Institution's National Air And Space Museum in Washington DC, USA.

2. Oldest tree fossil

The oldest fossils of trees found so far are about 385 million years old. Discovered in 2007 in southeast New York State, USA, they look like a bunch of bottlebrushes growing out of the top of a slender three story high trunk.

3. Oldest Egyptian mummy

The oldest Egyptian mummy is about 5,500 years old. It was made naturally when a body buried in the hot dry desert sand dried out quickly and was preserved. About 500 years later, Egyptians began making mummies by removing the organs and then treating the bodies with preservative substances before burial.

11 **Stone Age cave painting**
36,000 yrs old

2 **Tree fossil**
385 million yrs old

7 **Bristlecone Pine**
4,800 yrs old

3 **Egyptian mummy**
5,500 yrs old

4 **Tui Malila**
188 yrs old

Oldest

When Jeanne Calment died in 1997, she was the oldest person who has ever lived. She was 122 years old. When she was born, on February 21, 1875, many of the things that are common in our world today were unknown. It would be another year before Alexander Graham Bell invented the telephone and ten years before Karl Benz invented the automobile. However, she was a mere youngster compared to the world's oldest living tree, a Bristlecone Pine that's about 4,800 years old!

4. Animal with the longest lifespan

The oldest known animal was a giant tortoise called Tui Malila. It was given to the Royal Family of Tonga in the south Pacific by the famous English explorer, Captain Cook, in 1777. Tui Malila, which means King Malila in Tongan, lived for 188 years until its death in 1965.

13 Jericho
11,000 yrs old

12 Centennial
Light
109 yrs old

9 USS Constitution
213 yrs old

10 HMS Victory
245 yrs old

5 Diamond Sutra
1,142 yrs old

6 Icelandic clam
405 yrs old

13. Oldest continuously inhabited city

Jericho, in Jordan, is the world's oldest continuously inhabited city. People settled there because of the springs that flow down from the hills of Jerusalem and Ramallah, supplying fresh water for people, animals and crops. Archaeologists have found the remains of settlements on the same site going back 11,000 years to 9,000 BC.

12. Oldest light bulb

The oldest working light bulb has been lit almost non-stop since it was installed in the firehouse in Livermore, California, USA, in 1901. It's called the Centennial Light. The glass was blown into a bulb shape by hand and its glowing filament is made of carbon. It was lit all the time because it was used as a night-light over the fire trucks.

11. Oldest cave paintings

Cave paintings made by Stone Age people are very difficult to date, but the oldest cave paintings are thought to be about 30,000-36,000 years old. They were found in caves near Vallont-Pont-d'Arc in France and Verona, Italy.

10. Oldest warship still in commission

The oldest warship still in service is the British Royal Navy vessel, HMS Victory. She was launched in 1765 and famously fought at the Battle of Trafalgar in 1805 with Vice-Admiral Nelson in command. Today, she is in dry dock at Portsmouth Royal Naval Dockyard, and is open to the public.

9. Oldest commissioned warship still afloat

The oldest commissioned warship still afloat is the USS Constitution. She was launched in 1797.
The Constitution is a type of warship called a heavy frigate. She retired from active naval service in 1881.

8. Oldest rocks on Earth

The oldest rocks discovered on Earth so far were formed 4.28 billion years ago. They were found in 2008 on the shore of Hudson Bay, Canada, by scientists from McGill University in Montreal, Canada. Before this, the oldest known rocks were 4.03 billion years. They were found in Canada's Northwest Territories.

5. Oldest existing book

The oldest existing dated printed book is the Diamond Sutra. It's a Buddhist religious text printed in Chinese in 868AD. It is made of seven strips of paper pasted together to form a scroll 5 m (16 ft) long. Each strip was printed from a single carved block of wood.

6. Oldest clam

A clam dredged from the icy waters north of Iceland in 2007 is the world's longest-lived single animal. By counting the growth rings on its shell, researchers found it to be 405 years old. The clam was alive when it was taken from the water, but died soon afterwards.

7. Oldest living Tree

The oldest continuously growing tree is a Bristlecone Pine in California, USA, that's about 4,800 years old. A spruce tree in Sweden has a root system 9,550 years old, but the tree above ground is just a few years old – it's the latest tree to grow on the same root.

Lifespans

Mouse
1-2 yrs

Rabbit
5-10 yrs

Tiger
In the wild, tigers have a lifespan of about 10 years, but they can live to 26 years in captivity.

Cow
Cows can live for 25 years, but farm cows have much shorter lives. Dairy cows may live for only five years. Cattle raised for beef are usually killed around three years. The oldest cow on record, Big Bertha, died in 1993, at the age of 48.

Bison
The American bison is the biggest land animal in North America. It weighs up to a tonne (2,200 pounds). The bison's average lifespan in the wild is 18-20 years, but they can live a lot longer. Some are known to have lived for up to 40 years in captivity.

Mouse
A mouse lives 1-2 years in the wild, but longer as a pet.

Trout
4-6 yrs

Dog
6-15 yrs

Tiger
10-26 yrs

Monarch butterfly
Monarch butterflies that emerge as adults in the spring or early summer live only 2-4 weeks. Late summer adults live for up to 9 months.

Monarch butterfly
2 weeks - 9 months

Mayfly
1 day - 2 weeks

Earwig
1 year

Trout
Most trout live for 4-6 years, but some can reach 11 years.

Rabbit
Rabbits live for 5-10 years. Dwarf breeds outlive giant breeds.

Cow
25-48 yrs

Bison
18-40 yrs

Eagle owl
The Eagle Owl is the world's biggest owl. Found in mainland Europe and Scandinavia. They live for up to 40 years or perhaps 60 years in captivity.

Mayfly
Adult mayflies do not eat, so most live for just one day, although some live as long as two weeks.

Dog
Dogs have a lifespan of 6-15 years. The smallest breeds outlive the bigger breeds.

Polar bear
15-40 yrs

Earwig
Earwigs take 10 weeks to grow from egg to adult. Then they live a further 10 months, a total lifespan of about one year.

Chimpanzee
40-76 yrs

Rhinoceros
40-45 yrs

Hippopotamus
45-61 yrs

Humans
75-81 yrs

Eagle owl
40-60 yrs

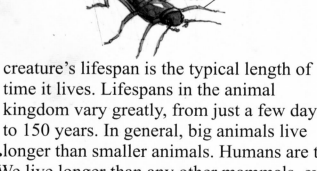

A creature's lifespan is the typical length of time it lives. Lifespans in the animal kingdom vary greatly, from just a few days to 150 years. In general, big animals live longer than smaller animals. Humans are the one exception. We live longer than any other mammals, even though many of them are bigger than us. Birds tend to live longer than mammals. Most wild animals live longer in captivity, where they have protection from predators, diseases and the extremes of weather.

Humans
The average lifespan for all humans is 66 years. People in rich countries live longest. Women usually live longer than men. The average US lifespan in 2008 was 81 years for women and 75 years for men.

Rhinoceros
The rhinoceros is the second biggest land animal. The black rhino and white rhino live in Africa. The Indian, Sumatran and Javan rhinos live in Asia. They all live for about 40 years in the wild and up to five years longer in captivity.

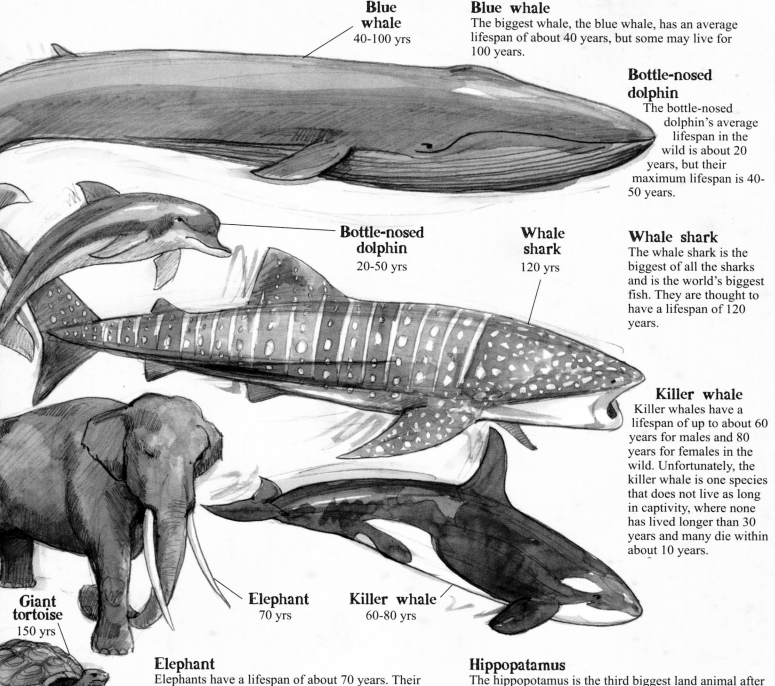

Blue whale
40-100 yrs

Bottle-nosed dolphin
20-50 yrs

Whale shark
120 yrs

Giant tortoise
150 yrs

Elephant
70 yrs

Killer whale
60-80 yrs

Blue whale
The biggest whale, the blue whale, has an average lifespan of about 40 years, but some may live for 100 years.

Bottle-nosed dolphin
The bottle-nosed dolphin's average lifespan in the wild is about 20 years, but their maximum lifespan is 40-50 years.

Whale shark
The whale shark is the biggest of all the sharks and is the world's biggest fish. They are thought to have a lifespan of 120 years.

Killer whale
Killer whales have a lifespan of up to about 60 years for males and 80 years for females in the wild. Unfortunately, the killer whale is one species that does not live as long in captivity, where none has lived longer than 30 years and many die within about 10 years.

Elephant
Elephants have a lifespan of about 70 years. Their lifespan depends on their teeth. The teeth move from the back of the mouth to the front as they wear down. Then the worn-down teeth fall out. When the last tooth falls out, an elephant cannot feed any longer and dies.

Hippopotamus
The hippopotamus is the third biggest land animal after the elephant and the white rhinoceros. Hippos live about 45 years in the wild or 50 years in captivity. The oldest was called Tanga. She died in a Munich zoo in at the age of 61.

Giant tortoise
The giant tortoise has the longest lifespan of any land animal. They can live for up to 150 years. Some have lived even longer than this. The oldest lived to be 188.

Polar bear
Polar bears have an average lifespan of 15-18 years in the wild, although a few tagged bears are known to have reached their early thirties. They live a few years longer in captivity, but it is very rare for any polar bear to live beyond the age of 40.

Chimpanzee
Chimpanzees live about 40-50 years in the wild, but can live longer in captivity. Some have lived beyond 60 years. The oldest known chimpanzee is Cheeta, the chimp that starred in Tarzan movies in the 1930s and 40s. In 2008, Cheeta was 76 years old!

Populations

The human population numbers more than 6 billion. It's vast, but it's nothing compared to the insect population of a billion billion, or about 170 million insects for every person! At the other end of the scale, the populations of some creatures are tiny. The worldwide population of amur leopards now amounts to just a few dozen.

Locusts

After heavy rain, a locust lays eggs. If the newly hatched locusts are close enough to touch, they begin to swarm. The biggest swarms of locusts can cover hundreds of square kilometres. A single swarm can have a population of more than 10 billion locusts. They eat their own weight in vegetation every day, destroying any crops they settle on.

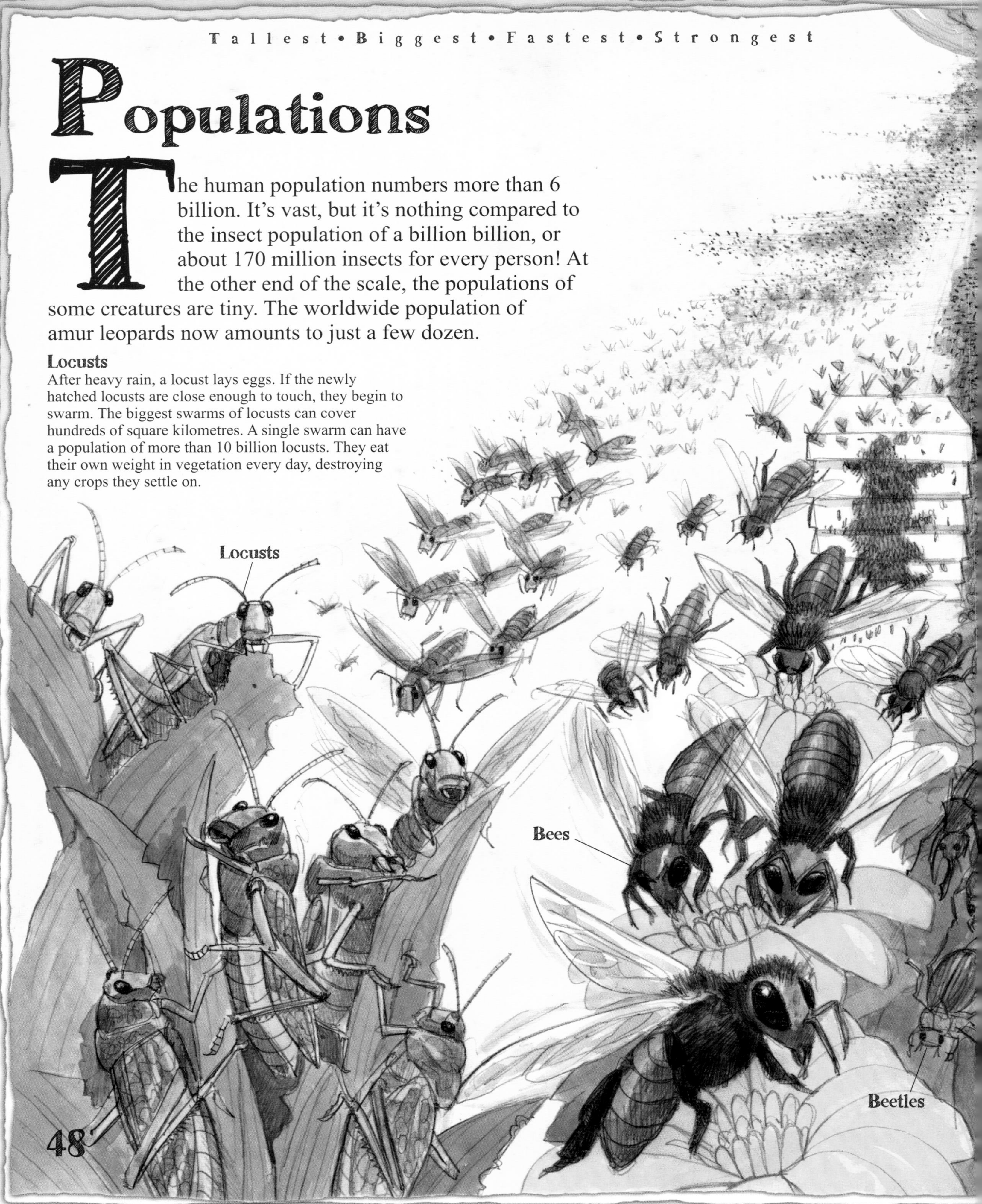

Locusts

Bees

Beetles

48

Beetles

Beetles are the most numerous creatures on Earth. A quarter of all animal species are beetles. Scientists have identified about 350,000 beetle species, but there may be more still to be found and named.

Bees

Bees live in close-knit colonies in the wild. The colony feeds on honey made by the bees from nectar they collected from flowers. Bee-keepers keep bee colonies in hives to produce honey for us. A hive is home to about 50,000 bees. Each hive has one queen, which lays about 200,000 eggs a year. Most of the eggs become female worker bees. A few become male drones.

Wildebeest

The migration of the Serengeti wildebeest is the biggest mammal migration on land. Wildebeest, or gnu, are big antelopes. They live in herds in East Africa. The largest herds live on the southern Serengeti plains in Tanzania. Every year 1.5 million wildebeest, 500,000 gazelles and 200,000 zebras make a 2,900 km (1,800 mile) round trip to Kenya's Masai Mara and back again to the southern Serengeti in search of food and water.

Humans

The human population reached 6.7 billion in 2008. It took up to 1804 for the population to grow to its first billion. It had doubled to 2 billion by 1927. It doubled again by 1974. The fastest population growth was in the 1960s. The rate of growth has slowed since then. Experts think the human population will grow to 9 billion by 2040-50 and it will have stopped growing by 2075 at less than 10 billion.

Wildebeest

Humans

Hottest

The hottest place in the USA is Death Valley in California. On July 10, 1913, a temperature of 56.7°C (134°F) was recorded there. It held the record for the highest temperature recorded anywhere on Earth for nine years. Other parts of Earth are far hotter than this. If you dig down into the ground, the temperature rises. At the bottom of the deepest mines in South Africa, nearly 4 km (2.5 miles) below the surface, the temperature is 55°C (131°F), almost as hot as Death Valley, and the mine has to be cooled. At the centre of the Earth, the temperature is approximately 6,000°C (10,800°F).

Africa

Africa is the hottest of all the continents. The highest temperature ever recorded on Earth was 57.8°C (136°F). It was measured in El Azizia in Libya on September 13, 1922. Dakol, in Ethiopia, has the highest average temperature of 34°C (94°F).

Indian Ocean

The oceans cover 71% of the Earth's surface. They are actually one continuous body of water divided into five oceans – the Atlantic, Pacific, Indian, Southern and Arctic oceans – together with smaller seas. The warmest of the five oceans is the Indian Ocean. It is also the third largest ocean.

Z-Machine

A remarkable X-ray generator called the Z machine at Sandia National Laboratories in New Mexico, USA, generates temperatures of 2 billion °C (3.6 billion °F) or more. That's more than 130 times hotter than the centre of the Sun! The Z machine works by sending 20 million amps of electricity through a set of wires thinner than human hairs. The wires vaporise instantly and the cloud of particles collapses. The particles fly together so fast and stop so suddenly that their energy is released as X-rays that produce incredibly high temperatures. When the machine is fired, lightning flashes all over it.

Supernova

The hottest place in nature is probably the centre of a supernova. A supernova is a massive exploding star. When the biggest stars run out of fuel and collapse, all the matter that falls inwards towards the centre of the star rebounds out into space. The star's brightness increases enormously. Inside a supernova, the temperature may reach an astonishing 100 billion degrees Celsius, or about 6,500 times hotter than the centre of the Sun.

Z-Machine

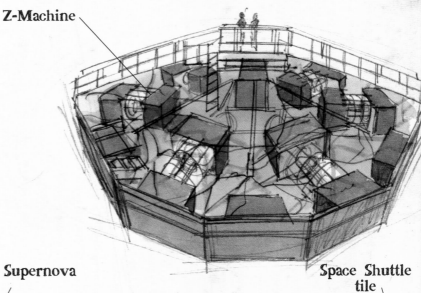

Supernova

Space Shuttle tile

Space Shuttle tile

As the Space Shuttle Orbiter re-enters the Earth's atmosphere at the end of a mission, it gets very hot. Temperatures here can reach 704°C (1,300°F). Without protection, it would burn up. The bottom of the Orbiter and most of its nose are covered with tiles called High-temperature Reusable Surface Insulation (HRSI). The tiles are made of glassy fibres with a black waterproof coating.

50

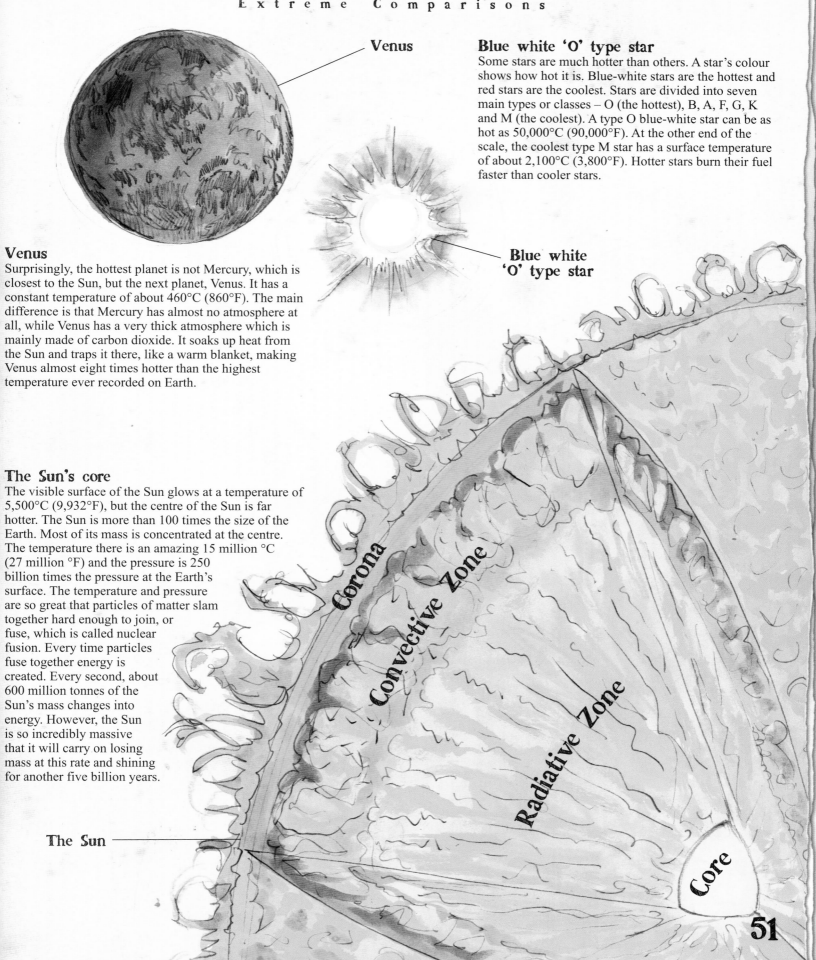

Venus

Surprisingly, the hottest planet is not Mercury, which is closest to the Sun, but the next planet, Venus. It has a constant temperature of about 460°C (860°F). The main difference is that Mercury has almost no atmosphere at all, while Venus has a very thick atmosphere which is mainly made of carbon dioxide. It soaks up heat from the Sun and traps it there, like a warm blanket, making Venus almost eight times hotter than the highest temperature ever recorded on Earth.

Blue white 'O' type star

Some stars are much hotter than others. A star's colour shows how hot it is. Blue-white stars are the hottest and red stars are the coolest. Stars are divided into seven main types or classes – O (the hottest), B, A, F, G, K and M (the coolest). A type O blue-white star can be as hot as 50,000°C (90,000°F). At the other end of the scale, the coolest type M star has a surface temperature of about 2,100°C (3,800°F). Hotter stars burn their fuel faster than cooler stars.

The Sun's core

The visible surface of the Sun glows at a temperature of 5,500°C (9,932°F), but the centre of the Sun is far hotter. The Sun is more than 100 times the size of the Earth. Most of its mass is concentrated at the centre. The temperature there is an amazing 15 million °C (27 million °F) and the pressure is 250 billion times the pressure at the Earth's surface. The temperature and pressure are so great that particles of matter slam together hard enough to join, or fuse, which is called nuclear fusion. Every time particles fuse together energy is created. Every second, about 600 million tonnes of the Sun's mass changes into energy. However, the Sun is so incredibly massive that it will carry on losing mass at this rate and shining for another five billion years.

51

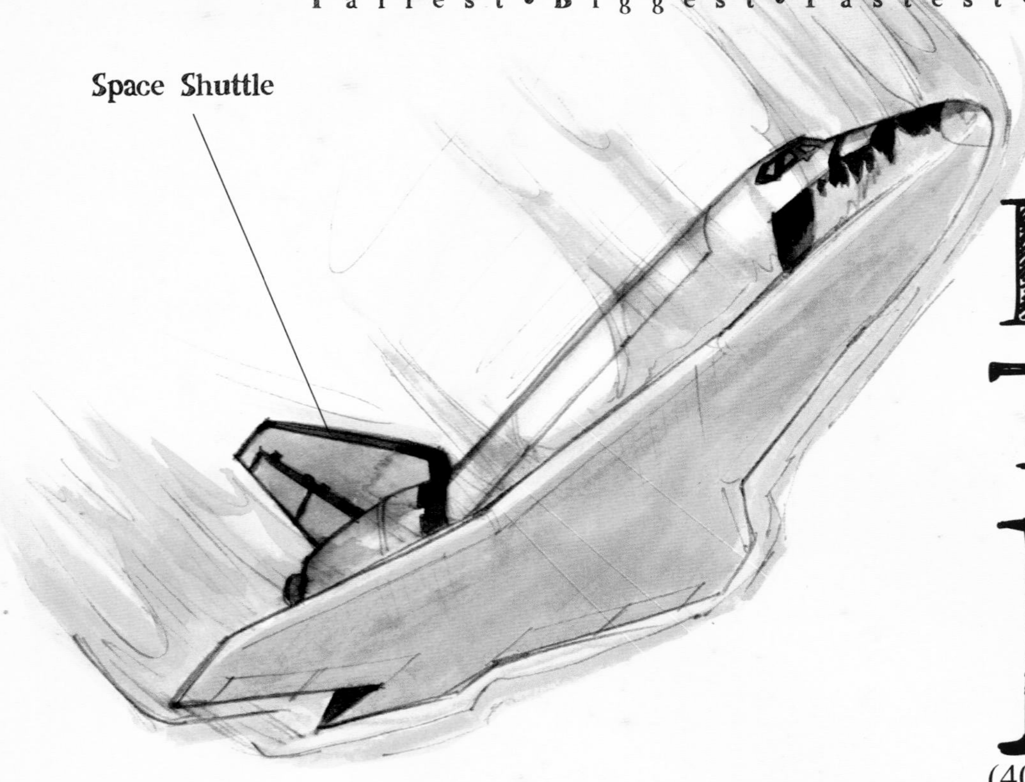

Space Shuttle

Lightning

High Temperatures

In the hottest parts of the world, the temperature can exceed 40°C (104°F). Water boils at 100°C (212°F). A kitchen oven cooks food at around 200°C (400°F). In industry, iron and steel are melted at over 1,000°C (1,830°F) to make into all shapes and sizes. An airliner's jet engines burn their fuel at 1,390°C (2,530°F). Nature can generate temperatures 20 times higher than this in lightning bolts, and 60,000 times higher than this in the centre of the Sun.

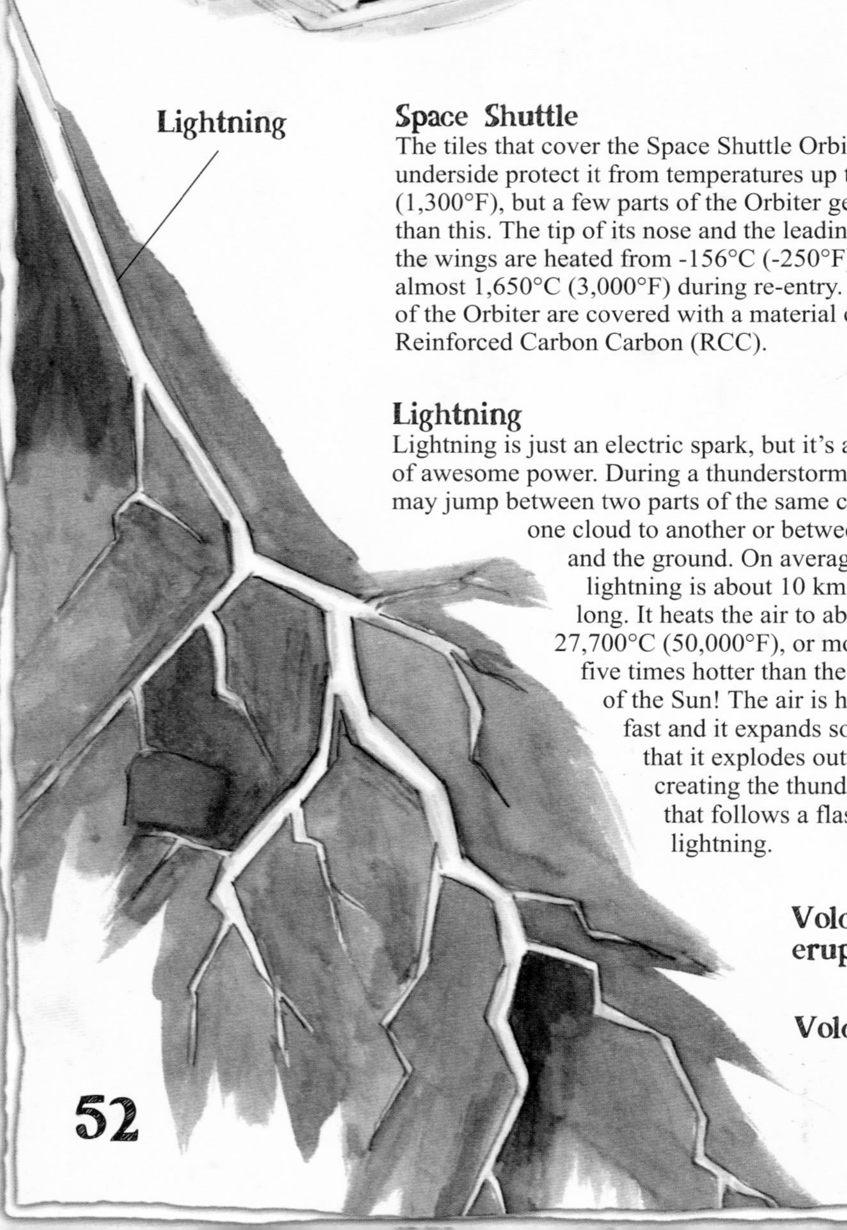

Space Shuttle
The tiles that cover the Space Shuttle Orbiter's underside protect it from temperatures up to 704°C (1,300°F), but a few parts of the Orbiter get even hotter than this. The tip of its nose and the leading edges of the wings are heated from -156°C (-250°F) in space to almost 1,650°C (3,000°F) during re-entry. These parts of the Orbiter are covered with a material called Reinforced Carbon Carbon (RCC).

Lightning
Lightning is just an electric spark, but it's a giant spark of awesome power. During a thunderstorm, lightning may jump between two parts of the same cloud, from one cloud to another or between a cloud and the ground. On average, a flash of lightning is about 10 km (6 km) long. It heats the air to about 27,700°C (50,000°F), or more than five times hotter than the surface of the Sun! The air is heated so fast and it expands so fast that it explodes outwards, creating the thunderclap that follows a flash of lightning.

Volcanic eruption

Volcano

Meteoroids

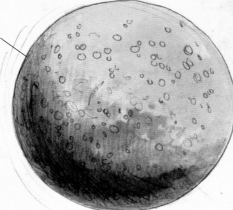

Mercury

The Sun

Meteoroids

Billions of pieces of rock plunge into the Earth's atmosphere from space every day. They are called meteoroids. Most are smaller than a grain of sand, the smallest are microscopic. They're called micrometeoroids. They drift down to the ground very slowly without burning up. Bigger meteoroids the size of a grain of sand heat up as they enter the atmosphere. They reach a temperature of 1,650° (3,000°F). That's hot enough to vaporise them. As they burn up, they produce a bright streak of light in the sky called a meteor or shooting star. Meteoroids bigger than a pebble may survive their fiery trip through the atmosphere and reach the ground. Meteoroids that hit the ground are called meteorites.

Mercury and the Sun

Mercury is the smallest of the eight planets in the solar system. Its orbit brings it as close as 47 million kilometres (29 million miles) from the Sun – three times closer than the Earth. The Sun heats Mercury's surface to 430°C (806°F). That's twice as hot as a kitchen oven and hot enough to melt lead and tin. When day turns to night, the temperature on Mercury's surface quickly plummets to -170°C (-274°F). The temperature drops fast, because Mercury has almost no atmosphere to hold onto the heat. Mercury spins on its axis once every 59 days and it takes 88 days to make one orbit of the Sun. The combination of the two means that a Mercury day, from one sunrise to the next, lasts 176 Earth days. One side of Mercury is roasted for 176 days and then it plunges below freezing and the other side is roasted for the next 176 days.

Nuclear explosion

Nuclear weapons are the most destructive weapons of all. They work by releasing vast amounts of energy locked up inside atoms. Nuclear power stations release energy from atoms in a steady stream over tens of years. A nuclear weapon releases all the energy in a fraction of a second. When a nuclear weapon explodes, up to half of the total energy is given out as heat. At the moment of detonation, the explosion produces lots of X-rays. The surrounding air within a few metres of the explosion soaks up the X-rays and its temperature soars, forming a fireball. The fireball isn't a normal ball of flame. It can be as hot as 10 million °C (18 million °F). The heat makes the fireball expand very quickly. It expands so fast that it squashes the surrounding air, producing a destructive blast wave. Hot air is lighter than cold air, so the fireball rises higher in the air. As it rises, it cools down and stops rising, forming the distinctive mushroom cloud.

Mushroom cloud

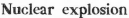

Nuclear Explosion

Volcano

When a volcano erupts, the lava that flows out is rock that is so hot that it has become liquid. The hottest lava, up to 1,200°C (2,200°F), produces the least violent eruptions. If the lava is cooler, no more than 1,000°C (1,830°F), it is thicker and so it's harder for gas trapped in the volcano to escape through it. The trapped gas builds up and bursts out, producing more violent eruptions. The coolest lava, up to 800°C (1,470°F), produces the most explosive and dangerous eruptions.

53

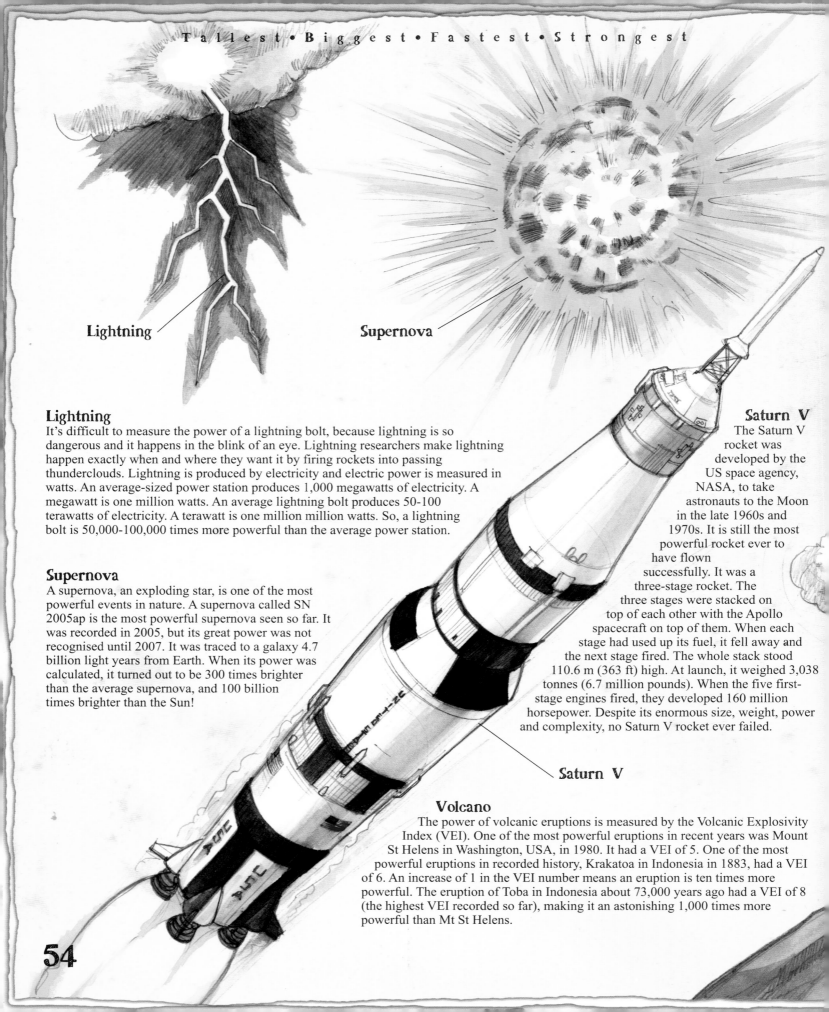

Lightning

Supernova

Lightning

It's difficult to measure the power of a lightning bolt, because lightning is so dangerous and it happens in the blink of an eye. Lightning researchers make lightning happen exactly when and where they want it by firing rockets into passing thunderclouds. Lightning is produced by electricity and electric power is measured in watts. An average-sized power station produces 1,000 megawatts of electricity. A megawatt is one million watts. An average lightning bolt produces 50-100 terawatts of electricity. A terawatt is one million million watts. So, a lightning bolt is 50,000-100,000 times more powerful than the average power station.

Supernova

A supernova, an exploding star, is one of the most powerful events in nature. A supernova called SN 2005ap is the most powerful supernova seen so far. It was recorded in 2005, but its great power was not recognised until 2007. It was traced to a galaxy 4.7 billion light years from Earth. When its power was calculated, it turned out to be 300 times brighter than the average supernova, and 100 billion times brighter than the Sun!

Saturn V

The Saturn V rocket was developed by the US space agency, NASA, to take astronauts to the Moon in the late 1960s and 1970s. It is still the most powerful rocket ever to have flown successfully. It was a three-stage rocket. The three stages were stacked on top of each other with the Apollo spacecraft on top of them. When each stage had used up its fuel, it fell away and the next stage fired. The whole stack stood 110.6 m (363 ft) high. At launch, it weighed 3,038 tonnes (6.7 million pounds). When the five first-stage engines fired, they developed 160 million horsepower. Despite its enormous size, weight, power and complexity, no Saturn V rocket ever failed.

Saturn V

Volcano

The power of volcanic eruptions is measured by the Volcanic Explosivity Index (VEI). One of the most powerful eruptions in recent years was Mount St Helens in Washington, USA, in 1980. It had a VEI of 5. One of the most powerful eruptions in recorded history, Krakatoa in Indonesia in 1883, had a VEI of 6. An increase of 1 in the VEI number means an eruption is ten times more powerful. The eruption of Toba in Indonesia about 73,000 years ago had a VEI of 8 (the highest VEI recorded so far), making it an astonishing 1,000 times more powerful than Mt St Helens.

Gamma ray burst

Gamma ray bursts are sudden outpourings of gamma rays from distant galaxies. They were discovered by accident in the 1960s when satellites launched to detect nuclear weapons tests picked up gamma ray bursts from space. A gamma ray burst can last from a few thousandths of a second to several minutes. Some of them are thought to come from massive stars as they collapse to form black holes. The most powerful gamma ray burst was detected by NASA's Swift satellite in 2008. Called GRB 080319B, it was traced to a galaxy 7.5 billion light years away. It was 2.5 million times brighter than the brightest supernova.

Volcanic eruption

Gamma ray burst

Most Powerful

Power is a measurement of how fast energy is changing from one form to another. A powerful light bulb is brighter because it changes electrical energy into light faster. A powerful vehicle is faster because its engine changes the energy in its fuel into motion faster. Mechanical power, the power of machines, is measured in horsepower. The unit of horsepower was invented by James Watt in 1782 so he could measure the power of his steam engines. The unit of electric power, the watt, was named after him. Horsepower is based on the rate at which a horse can typically work. The Space Shuttle's three main engines produce 37 million horsepower ... that's the work of 37 million horses!

Powerful Machines

The most powerful vehicles are rockets. Their power is measured in millions of horsepower. Most commercial transport vehicles are powered by diesel engines. These big, heavy engines are strong and reliable. Their power is measured in hundreds or thousands of horsepower. They use their power to transport heavy loads. Racing cars generate great power too, but they use it to go as fast as possible. To keep their weight down, they have lightweight petrol engines. Some racing car engines burn different fuels such as methanol. Dragsters, the most powerful competition cars, generate enormous power by burning a special fuel called nitromethane.

Saturn
V

Top Fuel
Dragster

Road train

Bulldozer

Bulldozers level land and move loose materials on large construction sites and in mining. They work by pushing a blade along the ground. The blade can be raised or lowered. Bulldozers are very heavy so they run on tracks to spread their weight over a bigger area. The biggest bulldozer in production today is the Komatsu D575. It is used mainly in mines in North America. It weighs 152.6 tonnes (336,420 pounds), or more than twice the weight of a US Army Abrams battletank! The power to operate such a heavy vehicle comes from a 1,150-horsepower diesel engine.

Road train

The biggest and heaviest road freight trucks in the world are Australian road trains. A road train is a 650-horsepower truck pulling up to six trailers. A whole road train may be 53 m (175 ft) long. Road trains carry goods, livestock and raw materials of all sorts across the vast empty plains of Australia. Steel bars called 'roo bars' on the front of the trucks are essential to protect them from collisions with wandering cattle and kangaroos.

Earth-moving truck

The biggest and most powerful trucks in the world are used in the mining industry. The biggest of these giants is the Liebherr T282B dump truck. It's so big that it can't be driven on ordinary roads. Each tyre is nearly 4 m (13 ft) high. It has six tyres – two at the front and four at the back. Each of these giant trucks can carry 363 tonnes of rock, weighing as much as 50 elephants! The power to carry such heavy loads is provided by the truck's massive 3,650 horsepower engine. The engine powers a generator, which makes electricity. The electricity powers electric motors, which turn the wheels.

Komatsu D575 bulldozer

Liebherr T282B

Top Fuel Dragster

Dragsters are designed to do one thing – to accelerate in a straight line as fast as possible. The fastest are Top Fuel dragsters. Powered by a 7,000 horsepower engine, they can accelerate to a top speed of 530 km/h (330 mph) in less than five seconds.

Saturn V

The Saturn V rocket launched a 45-tonne spacecraft, which is about the same weight that a road freight truck transports. To send its payload 400,000 km (250,000 miles) to the Moon, the Saturn V rocket had to be more than 500,000 times more powerful than the truck.

57

Pulling a Jumbo Jet

On October 15, 1997, strongman David Huxley strapped on a harness attached to a Qantas Boeing 747-400 airliner's nose wheel. Then he pulled the plane a distance of 91 m (298 ft 6 in) in 87 seconds. The feat took place at Sydney Airport, Australia.

Boeing 747-400

Weightlifter

Weightlifters are among the strongest people on Earth. Two weightlifting methods are used in competition – the 'snatch' and the 'clean and jerk'. The snatch involves lifting a weighted bar from the floor to above the weightlifter's head in one smooth movement. Heavier weights can be lifted by the clean and jerk, which involves lifting the bar to chest height first, and then above the head. Using the clean and jerk, Leonid Taranenko made the heaviest ever recorded lift of 266 kg (586 pounds) in Canberra, Australia on November 26, 1988.

Jumbo Jet

The Boeing 747-400 Jumbo Jet is the heaviest plane to be pulled along the ground by a human. A fully loaded Jumbo Jet weighs up to 397 tonnes (875,000 pounds) at take-off.

Leonid Taranenko: Heaviest Lift 266 kg (586 pounds)

Elephant

David Huxley: Pulled 187 tonnes (412,000 pounds) a distance of 91 m (298 ft 6 in) in 87 seconds.

Strongest

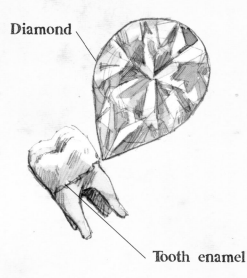

Diamond

Tooth enamel

Big animals such as lions and elephants are very strong, but some of the smallest creatures are even stronger. An animal's strength usually means how much it can lift or pull compared to its own body weight. An elephant can haul almost its own weight. The strongest humans, such as weightlifters, can lift more than their own weight. Some tiny beetles and mites can lift or pull 1,000 times their own weight! A human this strong would be able to lift an army tank weighing 63 tonnes (139,000 pounds)! Strength can be measured in other ways. The strength of a material can be measured by how hard it is. Teeth have to be very strong and hard to avoid being broken when they bite hard food.

Diamond

The diamond has been highly valued as a sparkling jewel for centuries, but diamond is also an extraordinary material. It is the hardest material found in nature. In fact, it is 140 times harder than the next hardest natural material, corundum, which forms rubies and sapphires.

Komatsu D575 bulldozer

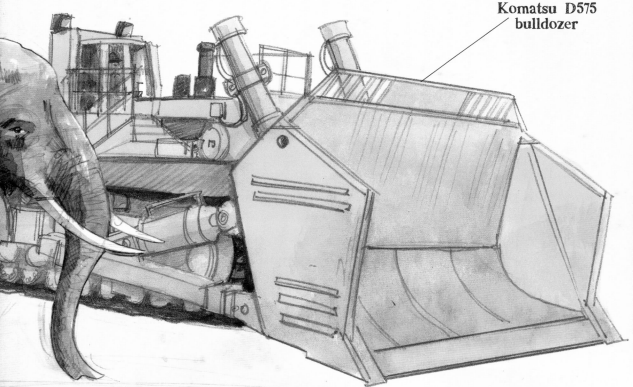

Tooth enamel

Tooth enamel is the strongest natural substance in the human body. A layer of enamel up to 2.5 millimetres (a tenth of an inch) thick covers the top of every tooth. It is made of a mineral called hydroxylapatite, the same substance found in bones.

Elephant

Elephants can lift and carry more weight than any other land animal. Some captive elephants are trained to work in dense forests where it is difficult for big machines to operate. They help to fell trees and then drag the trees out of the forest. The African elephant normally weighs about 7 tonnes and it can haul up to 5 tonnes. The smaller Asian elephant, also called the Indian elephant, can lift 700 kg (1,540 pounds) and haul 2 tonnes (more than 4,000 pounds) of wood a kilometre.

Bulldozer

Large bulldozers are fitted with blades that push up to about 35 cubic metres (45 cubic yards) of material along in front of them. As gravel and earth weigh about 1.5 tonnes per cubic metre, large bulldozers can push more than 50 tonnes. The record-breaking Komatsu D575 super dozer can push twice as much as this.

Glossary

altitude
The distance between an object and sea level.

antenna
A metal rod used to send and receive electromagnetic waves, such as radio waves.

astronomy
The study of the stars and the wider universe around us.

atom
The smallest unit of an element, regarded as a source of nuclear energy.

bottlebrush
An australian shrub with spiked flowers which look like they could be used to clean bottles.

borehole
A narrow shaft drilled into the ground, which can be used to extract natural gas or other materials from deep inside the Earth.

clocked
Recorded. Refers to the stopclock used to measure time.

colony
A group of the same type of animal or plant living or growing together.

diameter
The distance across the centre of a circle or sphere.

drone
A male bee, especially a honeybee, that is stingless, performs no work, and produces no honey. Its only function is to mate with the queen bee.

dwarf planet
An object orbiting the sun with a nearly round shape. Its gravity is not strong enough to clear objects from its neighbourhood, whereas a planet's is.

excavator
A machine which removes earth by digging into the ground.

flightless
With wings, but unable to fly.

foundation
A construction below the ground which supports the building above it.

gamma ray
An extremely powerful form of electromagnetic radiation.

glacier
A huge mass of ice flowing over land at an extremely slow pace.

hemispherical
The shape of half a sphere. Domed.

horsepower
A common unit of power. 1 horsepower is the amount of power needed to lift 33,000 pounds (about 15,000 kg) one foot (0.3 m) in one minute.

km/h
Short for 'kilometres per hour'. A measurement of speed based on how many kilometres an object will travel in the space of an hour.

light year
The distance that light can travel in one year, which is 9,460,730,472,580.8 km (or about 5,878,630,000,000 miles).

maglev
Short for magnetic levitation, a train which uses powerful magnets to lift the train slightly above the tracks.

mammal
A warm-blooded animal, such as a human being, dog or whale, the female of which produces milk to feed her babies.

manned
Has a person or crew of people aboard or inside it.

massif
A chain of mountains naturally linked together.

mast
A vertical pole used to send and receive information with an antenna. Often added to extremely tall buildings to slightly increase height.

Robert Wadlow
The tallest person who ever lived is Robert Pershing Wadlow, from Alton, Illinois, in the United States. He became the tallest person ever recorded when he was only 19, in 1937. He reached a height of 2.72 m (8 ft 11 in). He died on July 15, 1940 at the age of 22 from an infected blister.

Leonid Stadnyk
The tallest living person is Leonid Stadnyk, from Podolyantsi in Ukraine. He stands 2.57 m (8 ft 5.5 in) tall. Compared to him, a person of average height would be chest high.

Robert Wadlow

Average height

Leonid Stadnyk

mph
Short for 'miles per hour'. A measurement of speed based on how many miles an object will travel in the space of an hour.

nuclear fusion
A scientific process in which atoms are joined together to release huge amounts of energy. The use of nuclear power can be very dangerous.

observation deck
An elevated place where people can view an area or an event from a great height, often found in very tall towers.

orbit
The path a space object such as a planet or satellite takes around a much larger space object such as a star or bigger planet.

over-wintering
The part of migration in which an animal spends time in a warmer place to survive the cold winter.

payload
Something that is delivered or dropped off by an aircraft or spacecraft. Examples of cargoes referred to as a payload include rockets or satellites.

peninsula
A piece of land that is nearly surrounded by water but only just connected to the mainland.

predator
An animal which hunts other animals for food.

prey
An animal which is hunted by other animals for food.

re-entry
The process of re-entering the Earth's atmosphere from space.

satellite
An object in space that is much smaller than the object it orbits. A tv satellite orbits the earth but so does our moon. They are both satellites.

service ceiling
The highest altitude that an aircraft can reach.

shoal
A group of fish which remains together for social reasons. A school of fish, on the other hand, is a group of fish which group together and seem to think as one in order to avoid predators.

speed of sound
The speed at which a soundwave travels through a medium such as water or air. In dry air, the speed of sound is 1,236 km/h (768 mph).

spire
A tall tower on top of a building that tapers to a point at the top like a cone.

streamlined
Smooth enough or curved enough to resist air or water pressure and therefore able to travel faster.

submersible
A vessel such as a submarine, capable of operating and remaining underwater.

supersonic
Able to travel faster than the speed of sound.

tonne
A unit of weight equivalent to 1,000 kg (2,205 pounds).

trillion
A million million, or 1,000,000,000,000.

tropics
The area of Earth which is closer to the equator than it is to either the North or South Pole. The boundaries of this area are called the Tropic of Cancer in the northern hemisphere and the Tropic of Capricorn in the southern hemisphere.

tundra
An area of very low vegetative growth in cold parts of the world such as the Arctic.

wingspan
In aircraft or birds, the distance between the tip of one wing to the tip of the other.

x-ray
A form of electromagnetic radiation which can be used to see through certain substances such as flesh.

Index

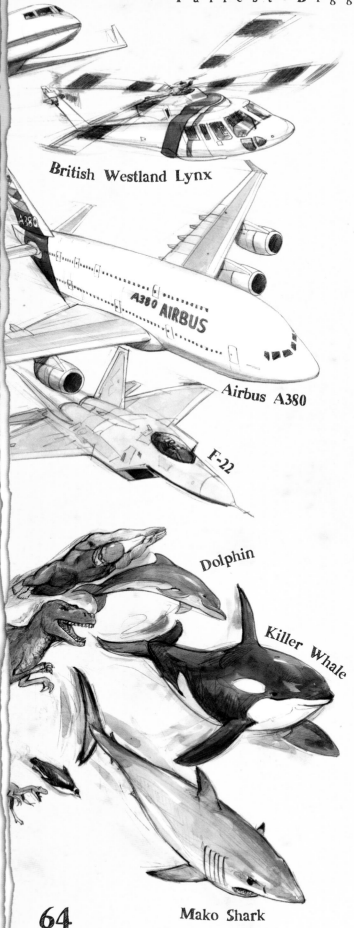

British Westland Lynx

Airbus A380

F-22

Dolphin

Killer Whale

Mako Shark

Strong Shapes

The shape of a structure is important, because some shapes are stronger than others. Arches have been used to make strong bridges for thousands of years. Domes have great structural strength too. Triangles make metal bridges and towers stronger. Spheres can resist enormous pressure.

Diamond
The triangles in the familiar diamond-shaped bicycle frame are what makes it so strong. They make a bike strong enough to support up to ten times its own weight.

Dome
St Paul's Cathedral in London is topped by one of the biggest cathedral domes in the world.

St Paul's Cathedral

Sphere
Alvin is a submersible, a small diving craft. The three-person crew sits inside a strong titanium sphere, which resists the pressure of the surrounding water.

Alvin submersible

Pont du Gard aqueduct

Bicycle frame

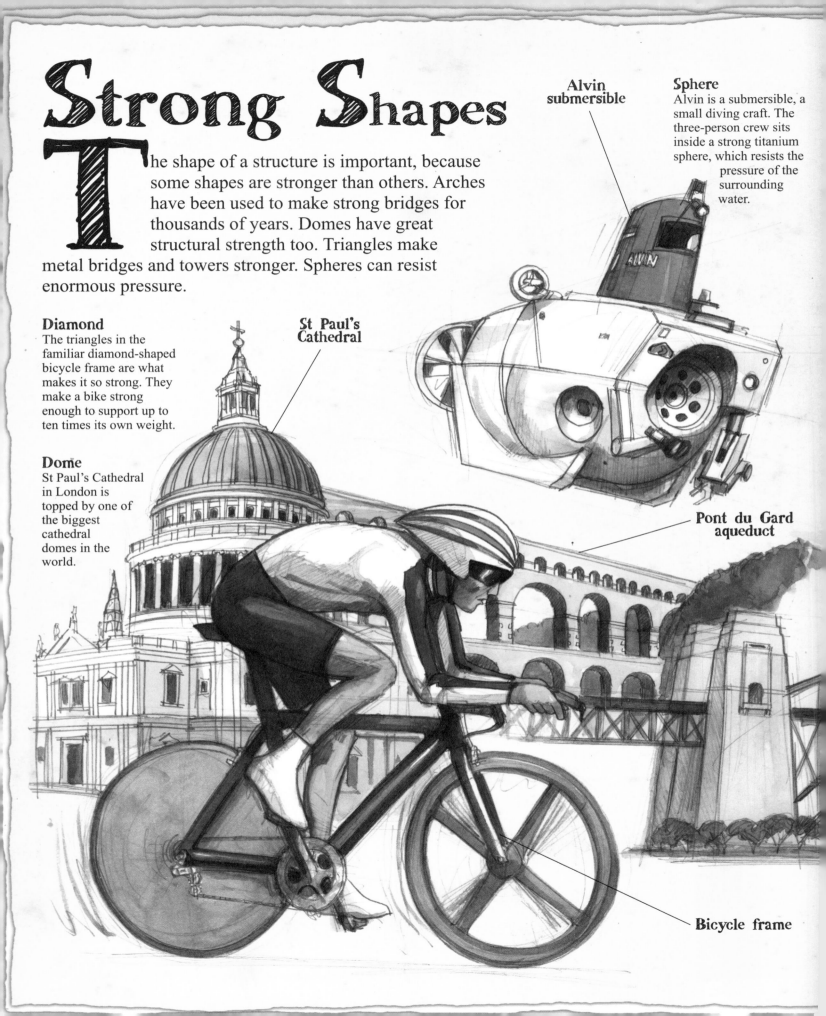